ALTERNATIVE SMALL PRESS PUBLISHING IN NEW ZEALAND

An introduction, with particular reference to the years
1969–1999

MICHAEL O'LEARY

Earl of Seacliff Art Workshop
Paekākāriki
© Michael O'Leary 2001

A thesis submitted to the Victoria University of Wellington in fulfillment of the
requirements for the degree of Master of Arts in English, 2001

First published in 2007 by Steele Roberts Publishers, Box 9321 Te Whanganui-a-Tara,
Wellington.

Abstract

This thesis is on small press literary publishing in New Zealand in the last thirty years. The method of information gathering is mainly primary resource material in the form of questionnaires sent to those directly involved as small press publishers during that period. The overwhelming response to the twenty five questionnaires (twenty three positive replies, the two who couldn't respond gave full support for the project) shows a need in the small press fraternity to give their view and to have their contribution to New Zealand literature more broadly acknowledged.

The brief historical background to the history of literary publication in New Zealand since 1830 briefly touches on the lack of Māori small press publishers, seemingly non-existent until the advent of Huia Publishers in 1991. Huia being one of my respondents makes the issue of Māori publishing relevant to small presses in New Zealand, both in an historical and contemporary sense.

That the 1960's cultural 'revolution' influenced the small press movement is a major theme, a fact borne out time and again from the primary source material. This thesis recognises people who dedicate so much time and resources to ensure that our literature is vibrant and alive. The protagonists from the 1960's era who had a profound effect on the 'youth culture' like Bob Dylan and John Lennon are shown to have had a significant influence by simply showing that "You can do it." That waiting for official sanction was not necessary - a major underlying catalyst to those involved in small presses.

The respondents challenge the myth that self-publishing is somehow inferior, asserting that small press publishing allows the artist control over their work, and that this is a positive and desirable thing.

Acknowledgments

I would like to thank my supervisors Paul Millar who realised the significance of the original idea, and Jim Traue who has patiently seen me through the process of making it into a reality. I would also like to thank those who supported me with helpful comments and encouragement and general backup which makes a project like this possible. These include Niel Wright, Alan Loney, Moana Cleverley, Clare O'Leary, Trevor Reeves, Toby McAuslan, Gregory O'Brien, Alister Taylor, Wendy Harrex, John Quilter, Rowan Gibbs, Aroha and Te Amoraki, Bill Dacker, Con O'Leary, Mary-Jane Duffy, Anna-Marie O'Brien, Mark Amery, Rose McAuslan, Malcolm Murchie, Winsome Aroha, Kathleen Coleridge, Don Polly, Kim Worthington, Graham Lindsay and Brian Opie.

Special thanks are due to all the small press publishers who took the time to answer the questionnaire and help with the bibliographies of their presses.

An Introduction to an Introduction

In presenting this thesis for examination my concern is to put on record the contribution to our literature made by what Alan Loney refers to as ' "the other tradition" in New Zealand.'[1] The approach of this work to the subject of 'alternative' publishing may be in some respects unorthodox, in the sense that a questionnaire sent to participants is usually not correct procedure for an English degree, but is rather the domain of the social sciences where strict protocol and procedures are adhered to.

However, this thesis was always intended as an 'introduction' to the subject. It is therefore entirely appropriate that the main thrust and achievement of the present document is focused on the presses themselves and the people who were involved in alternative publishing. It is hoped that the data collected in the often candid responses to the questions and the information provided in the bibliographies which accompany each of the publisher's replies will be of assistance to future scholars.

Many of the principal protagonists in this survey are getting to an age where other interests and responsibilities, loss of memory, or even mortality itself threatens to make such intimate details which emerge from the questionnaires almost impossible to recreate if future studies were to be attempted. Unlike past generations who left behind diaries and correspondence, the communications revolution in the twentieth century means that many details now go unrecorded. Where someone like Keats or Wordsworth may have written to a publisher in relation to aspects concerning publication of a new volume of poetry, nowadays a poet will probably do the same thing by telephone or other electronic form of communication. It is highly unlikely that future scholars will be able to trace such phone calls, and even e-mails may be considered too ephemeral for preservation by many.

The question of what constitutes an 'alternative small press' and why some publishers were chosen to answer the questionnaire is important. As this study is seen by its author as the beginning of further research, rather than a definitive academic treatise, much of its methodology is tentative. In fact it is more akin to an oral history project than a conventional English thesis, in that its primary aim is to capture the thoughts and ideas of the participants. Its value may be seen in the light of the death of one of the founders of a press which it was hoped could be included in the study: Don McKenzie of Wai-te-ata Press died during the preparation of this thesis and it was thought inappropriate to send the questionnaire to anyone else because it is now a distinctly different operation than when McKenzie began it. People such as Bob Gormack (Nag's Head), Niel Wright (Original Books), Bernard Gadd (Hallard Press), Oz and Ruth Kraus (Brick Row) — all people who have contributed to small press publication in this country over the past thirty years — are at an age where their motivations and ideals could be lost to the public record.

The questionnaire was designed and distributed to collect a sample of the prevailing types of small press publishing and writing during the period 1969 to 1999. In no way does it claim to be definitive or even representative of any particular movement or tradition. Of the twenty six questionnaires sent to small press publishers only three could not reply. Those three (Alister Taylor, Quentin Wilson of Hazard Press, Wendy Harrex of New Women's

Press) all supported my project and expressed interest in replying but were too busy with other work to meet my deadline.

However, a preliminary bibliography of their presses is included in the Supplementary Bibliographies section to give something of an indication of their contribution. To receive a return rate of twenty three out of twenty six replies from such a group of busy people is an indication of how these publishers felt about the importance of this project and how overlooked by the literary establishment some of them felt they were. Again, this written form of oral history has proved its worth.

So what is "alternative" publishing, and who are the "establishment" they are providing an alternative to? These questions are not easily answered and there appears to be many cross-overs between several of the publishers who responded. Broadly there is three types of perceived establishment publishers: commercial, literary and academic. Other factors influence such classifications. For example, Huia Publishers, who on the face of it seem to be straight commercial publishers, are alternative because they were established in the face of what was a perceived Pakeha establishment of publishers. As Robyn Bargh states, in the response to the first question about becoming involved in publishing, she "set up Huia Publishers in 1991 because I considered that New Zealand literature did not adequately represent the views, values and attitudes of Māori people I knew."[2] Thus it is quite fitting that Huia should be included in a work on alternative publishing; and with a kaupapa which states that works published by Huia Publishers "have to contribute in some way to the development of Māori writers or literary thought" [3] her fight against the Pakeha 'establishment' seems set to continue.

Another form of alternative versus establishment publishing can be seen in the presses founded during the drive in the seventies for equality between men and women by members of the women's liberation movement. Wendy Harrex of the New Womens Press was a prime mover in this field. Another important woman in the struggle to have women's work taken seriously is poet Heather McPherson of the Spiral Collective. Early on in her career she realised that she would have to take up the fight against the male establishment when she told Leo Bensemann, then editor of ***Landfall***, that she had a collection of poetry and would he look at them. "I mentioned that I had become a feminist. He said that Rita Cook - Rita Angus - had become a feminist 'but it didn't do her any good either.'" [4]

In the face of attitudes like this (even though Bensemann said her poems were publishable) the battle lines were drawn. McPherson states that after joining a group to fight for homosexual law reform "with a number of talented women artists in the group, with their stories being turned down for publication or by art galleries, I thought I would rather be working with/for women artists." [5] Thus the Spiral Collective was formed to a provide an alternative to the male literary and artistic establishment.

Traditionally, however, when speaking about established versus alternative publishing, definitions need to be addressed. This is difficult, especially when talking about small press publishing in a diminutive market such as New Zealand. Two major categories emerge from the questionnaire respondents. Firstly, presses such as Alan Loney's Hawk Press are dedicated to a type of production of literature using aesthetics as a guiding force for both presentation and selection of material. Loney states that "there was worthwhile poetry being written that was not getting published, and that books that were being published could be better designed and produced than was the case at the time." [6] This type of operation is often seen as the genuine expression of a "small press" as their production methods include hand-setting of text and art house design standards.

Secondly, there are what is termed non-commercial presses such as One-Eyed Press and Amphedesma Press. These often arise out of situations where someone knows of a piece of writing that they think should be published but is unlikely to be touched by any commercial operation. These presses employ whatever technology is expedient to get the job done, hopefully at the lowest cost.

C.E.G. Moisa's One-Eyed Press illustrates this. Moisa recalls "Mark [Williams] one day [saying] that he would have liked me to illustrate a book of poems that he was hoping to publish." [7] After looking around at options Moisa decided on approaching "a fast print place (IMPRINT) down where the bus depot is in down town Auckland." [8] He got a quote, published ***Abecedary*** and One-Eyed Press was born.

Meanwhile, at the same time twelve thousand miles away, Bill Manhire and Kevin Cunningham were engaged in similar activities establishing Amphedesma Press. Manhire explains how they used "office facilities (mostly the electric typewriters) to prepare photo-ready texts, and took them off to a local fast copy shop (these were just getting in London in the early 70's). We bought our own cover card - mostly in the Tottenham Court Road at a place called (I think) Paperchase." [9]

I have tried to allude to a few of the many 'alternatives' in NZ publishing in this short introduction. Several others will reveal themselves either through the text of the thesis or in the responses to the questionnaires. Whether it be alternatives in technology, philosophy or literary taste and judgement it is hoped that the present document will provide a starting point for further study and discussion on the field of alternative publishing within the wider world of publishing and writing produced in this country. The fact that I have chosen to present this material as a university thesis may appear incongruous to some. The main reason for doing this work within an academic framework is to have the endeavours of all these small press publishers recorded as part of a public archive.

---

1. Questionnaire response - Hawk Press, Q9, p110.
2. Questionnaire response - Huia Publishers, Q1, p117.
3. Questionnaire response - Huia Publishers, Q3, p117.
4. Questionnaire response - Spiral Collective, Q1, p164.
5. Questionnaire response - Spiral Collective, Q1, p166.
6. Questionnaire response - Hawk Press, Q1, p108.
7. Questionnaire response - One-Eyed Press, Q1, p132.
8. Questionnaire response - One-Eyed Press, Q1, p132.
9. Questionnaire response - Amphedesma Press, Q6, p62.

Chapter One

IN THE BEGINNING WAS THE (PRINTED) WORD

"The history of small, private presses in this country is also (largely) the history of our literature."[1] While particularly referring to poetry this quote from Michael Gifkins' 1990 'Bookmarks' column in the ***New Zealand Listener*** graphically states the case for the important place small press publishing has in the literary culture of New Zealand Aotearoa. Expanding this further, it is true to say that without the existence of such presses many of our writers, both well-known and obscure, may never have had the opportunity of being published authors, especially at the fledgling time of their career. This thesis will endeavour to prove that our literature would be the poorer if such publishers didn't exist, that we may have little literary industry or culture without them.

The wing-and-a-prayer, number-8-wire, shoe-string budget, do-it-yourself Kiwi approach to the practicalities of publishing in a mini-market environment has its genesis in the very first printing done here. In 1830 the Rev W. Yate published his ***Catechism in Māori***, a six page tract of which it has been said "their struggle with press, ink and paper must have been heroic, and certainly proved disastrous."[2] The effort in labour, artistry and resources in book production, both printing and publishing, in this country from these early times up to the present day can often be seen in such terms.

The second printing press arriving in New Zealand was brought to dry land by lashing two Māori canoes together, a dangerous and precarious practice and one which serves as a useful image for future enterprises in the publication of works through to the present day, as our small presses negotiate the waves and tides of small markets, difficult distribution, high unit cost of production, prejudice against buying local works by both the public and booksellers, and lack of academic appraisal.

However, it is these very difficulties which ensure in some unspoken way that the people drawn to the small press fraternity, who are often tough, rugged individualists, thrive on the non-conformities and insecurities inherent in this mercurial activity. The majority of them are poets and writers themselves and therefore have a natural and intimate insight into the very real problems of becoming a writer, and more importantly, getting published in New Zealand. As Alan Loney of Hawk Press intimated to me in a recent telephone interview that if we hadn't done it (i.e. published our own and our fellow writers' works) ourselves, probably nobody would have.[3]

It is with these things in mind that we can look back over the historical development of small press publication in New Zealand and trace the philosophical as well as the practical lineage which follows from the first endeavour of Yate in 1830 through to the present day. Indeed, what will become increasingly clear is that most, if not all, publishing in New Zealand can be considered under the banner of "small publishing" and it is this fact which underpins the whole industry in this country.

To define what constitutes a "small press" is as difficult a task as it is to pigeon-hole the individuals involved. Indeed, Cave in his book **Private Presses** suggests that "waywardness and eccentricity are in the traditions of the material".[4] He adds that such presses are unofficial presses which do not run for profit, but rather produce literary works of an aesthetic nature for a small or restricted audience.

It will be seen as this work progresses into the post-1969 period, which is eventually its main concern, that Cave's idea is apposite and generally fits the period and people as a definition. However, before this arises it is important to enter into a general historical background to small press publishing over a period of 170 years in New Zealand.

New Zealand small press publishing falls into three broad, distinct periods, each of which is a continuation of, and a separation from, the period which preceded it. The first section of time covers almost exactly the first century of publishing in New Zealand, that is 1830 to 1930, give or take a year or two. The second covers the years 1930 to 1970, the period when New Zealand publishing came of age in the literary sense. Finally, the time from 1970 to the present day, which has seen an explosion of small press publishers experimenting with many different forms of typography, technology and literary production.

As we have seen in the Yate experiment the birth of New Zealand 'literature' was not an easy one. Indeed, the first few years of printing / publishing in our country was largely defined by and confined to political and religious tracts of one form or another (particularly in relation to Māori language works). One could argue that this was small press publishing at its rawest edge, shaping and moulding the intellectual life of a young nation without anything to compare it to previously. It was practical, propagandist, and altogether concerned with the arguments involved in setting up a new society.

In December 1834 William Colenso arrived in Aotearoa. Not only was he a printer-craftsman, but he was an innovative and ingenious improviser who built a working press out of the incomplete machinery he was given to work with. On "the 17th of February 1835 the proofs were pulled of the first 'book' published in this country, a sixteen page version of ***The Epistles (of Saint Paul) to the Ephesians and the Philippians,***"[5] of which two thousand copies were made. It was the machine that printed this work which had been brought ashore with the help of the two Māori waka.

Colenso lost a lot of the original cold type overboard, which made an already tough task even more so, given the lengthy delays in getting replacements and his overseas suppliers' lack of knowledge of the requirements for Māori language printing. Also, he employed and developed several Māori apprentices to assist in the production of his first book, which had its own set of problems.

Generally, however, Māori people took very readily to the printed word and it is an unfortunate aspect of the history of presses in New Zealand that more Māori literary publishing houses have not been part of the development of New Zealand literature, until recently with the advent of concerns such as Huia Publishers. This might be an indication of just how badly affected by war, poverty and the policy of assimilation, the indigenous people were in the early days of New Zealand.

With the printing of the New Testament in Māori, **Ko te Kawenata Hou**, in 1837, Colenso steadily increased the volume of his production. By 1843 he had produced over sixty items, ranging in number per book from one hundred to twenty thousand copies. Colenso used his press to come to Governor Hobson's aid by printing a circular in 1840 exhorting the Māori Chiefs to attend the meeting at Waitangi, which would lead to the signing of the treaty. He also printed two hundred copies of the **Treaty of Waitangi.**

There was an early acceptance in New Zealand of the notion of what would later be disparagingly referred to as "vanity press" publication. For example, it has been acknowledged that most early works such as political pamphlets "were certainly paid for by the authors."[6] It was not until 1852 that the first book of poetry was written and published in this country. Entitled **New Zealand Minstrelsy**, it was by the poet William Golder who "followed the old balladmonger's tradition of personally canvassing for subscribers and hawking his books for sale."[7]

While not significant as a literary work **Minstrelsy** does mark the beginning of the long struggle involved in publishing poetry in New Zealand Aotearoa The fact is that many such works are published and sold in a similar manner by small presses even today.

This was also the case with one of the most famous and ornate literary publications of the first hundred years of printing and self-publishing in New Zealand. While Thomas Bracken's ***Musings in Maoriland*** was the result of an elaborate printing job carried out in Leipzig, and bearing the imprint of Arthur T. Keirle of Dunedin, it was "probably essentially self-published."[8] Certainly, a hint of the shapes of things to come, and an indication that not much has changed in the publication difficulties of poetry production and distribution in New Zealand from 1890 to 1990 and beyond.

As New Zealand society developed after the Treaty of Waitangi had been signed, printers began to appear in ever increasing numbers. Newspapers, political and religious tracts, and provincial propagandists began using the emerging print media to put forth their various concerns. One of the least known and acknowledged areas of this was the way Māori used the written word. Most historians see the Land Wars, for example, in terms of the physical acts of warfare. However, Māori people, whose enthusiasm for reading and the written word had been fuelled by the missionaries with their zealous productions of Bibles and other religious writings, had begun to realise the power of the printed word in their increasing struggles with the Crown and the settlers. In 1861 a Waikato Chief, Waata Kukutai, set up a press in Auckland known as ***Ko Aotea.***

Ko Aotea (The Māori Recorder) proved to be too suspect and subversive for the Government and in 1865 C.O.B. Davis, a long time fighter for Māori causes who had encouraged Kukutai to set up the press, was charged with seditious libel for the publication of a leaflet which was not even his. Such an over-reaction to an incident like this shows how sensitive the authorities were when dealing with Māori publishing.

One reason for such disquiet was possibly the fact that a few years before in 1858 two young Māori from Waikato, Wiremu Toetoe Tuaone and Te Hamara Perehau Paraone, had been to Austria to learn printing. After leaving they were presented by their hosts at the Imperial Royal Printing House with a press.

On their return to Aotearoa they began practising their trade, firstly at Mangere in 1860 and later at Ngaruawahia in 1862. They established ***Te Hokoio***, a pro-Kingitanga newspaper, which circulated up to ten issues between June 1862 and May 1863. The two young men might well have been influenced by the revolutionary ideas which were prominent in Europe at the time of their visit and transported them back to the situation of their own people. If so, their views would have coincided with the growing tension in New Zealand over issues of land and sovereignty.[9]

The Government tried to counter this publication by bringing out their own newspaper **Te Pihoihoi Mokemoke i Runga i Te Tuami** under the stewardship of John Gorst. However, a group from Maniapoto carried out their own form of censorship by seizing the press and taking lock, stock and cold type back to Ngaruawahia for their own use. It obviously had become a dangerous business this dealing with the printed word. It could even be surmised, given the laws of tapu and mana that after the land wars of the 1860's and 1880's many Māori people felt that not only had they lost their land, but also the intellectual and political power which the printed word had seemed to promise.

However, Apirana Ngata has a different interpretation of why Māori people didn't take to the printed word and benefit from it. He asserts that "'education through the ear, conveyed by artists and interpretation and gesticulation' was preferred by the 'genius of the race' to 'mute transference through the eyes'."[10] Thus, Ngata implies that Māori were not suited to learning from books because of their long-standing oral tradition of passing on knowledge.

While there was a later Kingitanga newspaper, **Te Pakio Matariki**, which lasted from 1891 to 1902, the Māori publishing presses never really recovered, and even today it is only Huia Publishers who are dedicated to the exclusive publishing of Māori literature. A further consideration in relation to Māori writers is that there may be many unpublished and untranslated manuscripts. According to Otago historian Bill Dacker, whom I interviewed recently,[11] these still remain in whanau or hapu hands and have often not been disturbed since the writer last touched them over a century ago. These taonga remain part of the unseen legacy left over from the land wars and exemplify the lack of trust and loss of mana engendered by the loss of land. Further to this Dacker, in his

1994 publication ***Te Mamae me te Aroha***, offers evidence of a printing press purchased by Ngai Tahu in the 1860's which lay unused for many years as the people grappled with poverty and the trauma which befell them. With the death of Tiramorehu, the main visionary behind the printing press for Ngai Tahu, in 1883 at Moeraki, so the dream of the tribe having its own voice in the new world died also. "Sadly, he did not live to establish a printing press at Moeraki as he had hoped."[12] This may have been the case in other tribal areas also. Again this may offer some understanding of why there was no substantial Māori literature up until the last twenty years or so, beyond the 'oral tradition' explanation proffered by Ngata, a possibility that clearly warrants further investigation.

In the phone conversation previously mentioned Dacker cited a document (Beattie MS 181, Notebook 4, Sections 10,11,12) held in the Hocken Library in Dunedin, in which Herries Beattie met someone who had seen the printing press at Moeraki on which Tiramorehu hoped to establish a Ngai Tahu newspaper. He also planned to write and print his own history of the tribe according to the source. Tiramorehu is said to have slept in the same room as the press and to have built a Whare Parehe (Press House) especially to shelter his precious machine.

Dacker also spoke of a woman, Vivienne Leonard, who he interviewed during his gathering of oral history material. The woman said she remembered seeing the remnants of the press outside Uenuku, the meeting house at the Moeraki Marae. The source of the interview is the Oral History section in the McNab Room of the Dunedin Public Library: (He Whanau a ka Korerorero - OMH9).

After the wars of the 1860's New Zealand settled into developing a nation along the lines that the Pakeha victors had in mind all the time. The empire builders with their large presses such as the daily newspapers in the main metropolitan areas like the ***Otago Daily Times*** and the ***New Zealand Herald*** began to dominate. Also, there was the development of the Government Printers and up to the 1930's publishing in New Zealand seemed to be largely dominated by the concerns of commerce and politics.

The writing which did appear during the post-land war period was often the writing or re-writing of the history of New Zealand by the Pakeha victors. Frederick Manning's **Old New Zealand**, George Grey's **Polynesian Mythology** and Edward Tregear's **The Aryan Māori** look back on a great, noble race of people as though they were an anthropological study of a long ago culture. H.W. Williams listed over a hundred printers, by far the majority of whom were Pakeha, who had published and printed in te reo Māori in his book **Bibliography of Printed Māori to 1900.** Williams himself was a fine printer, working from Gisborne on his Te Rau Press between 1901 and 1913 when he was the Bishop of Waiapu.

Literary publishing was almost non-existent and the few novelists and poets' main outlet was in newspapers until the 1930's and later, even though H.B. Stoney's **Taranaki: a Tale of the War** "sometimes erroneously referred to as the first New Zealand novel"[13] had been published by the Auckland publisher and printer W.C.Wilson as far back as 1862.

Meanwhile, in the general population of the new colony printing and publishing began to gather momentum: "Printing presses were stowed in the first emigrant ships as a matter of course".[14] But it wasn't until a generation after Colenso, from 1864, that Robert Coupland Harding began to make an impact. He belonged "to a tradition of marrying print and writing"[15] which throughout the history of the printed word in New Zealand is time and again looked to and followed. Many of the writers involved in publishing have also been hands-on people when it comes to the production of a book and in doing so have had far more control over the aesthetic and other aspects of the book they produce. This will become clear as a motivating factor later on, in particular with people like Alan Loney of Hawk Press and Warwick Jordan of Hard Echo Press, along with Glover and Lowry et al.

Even the first real literary publication which could be considered as Government funded,[16] (and which was to lay the foundation for state patronage of the arts in more ways than one) John White's **Ancient History of the Māori**, was essentially an unwieldy and melancholic attempt to document what was seen, obviously officially now, as a dying race.

Literary publishing was largely done by the periodicals and newspapers (which had an over-capacity due to investment in large printing plant technology) during this period, which would publish local short stories and poetry. "According to Hocken the first to attempt a monthly magazine in New Zealand"[17] was George Chapman, an Auckland bookseller, in 1862. This was followed by ***The Southern Monthly Magazine*** in 1863 and ***The Fortnightly Review*** in 1865.

However, the literary and intellectual climate at the time in New Zealand had been described quite unequivocally by Samuel Butler in a letter to his father, "It does not do to speak about John Sebastian Bach's 'Fugues' or pre-Raphaelite pictures."[18] Meanwhile, Harding continued to build on his earlier work, publishing a journal from 1887 to 1897 named ***Typo***, along with several other books and pamphlets. Chapman and Brett (owner of the ***Auckland Star***) continued with small-scale but planned publishing of local material, and a Wanganui printer, A.D. Willis, began to put out local histories, fictional sketches, a comic annual and a free-thought review. He also produced Tregear's ***The Māori Race,*** as well as a number of school text books.

It is around this time that a name which would tower over New Zealand publishing for many years first appeared. In 1882 the imprint of Whitcombe and Tombs began to be seen on school books. From this time until the next phase of New Zealand publishing, which would begin around the 1930's, this partnership between the literate, ambitious and enterprising George Whitcombe and George Tombs, the jobbing printer working with antiquated equipment in Cathedral Square, Christchurch, and their descendants, completely dominated the indigenous book production and book selling industry in New Zealand.

Satchell's ***Maorilander***, the original ***Zealandia***, ***The Triad***, and several other short-lived periodicals were among the few outlets for writers, apart from Whitcombe and Tombs' literary book production, from the 1880's to the 1930's. By the thirties Whitcombe and Tombs began to fall victim to their own success, that is "their conservatism had come to induce complacency and dullness."[19] However, there is an interesting link between the first phase of New Zealand publishing and the second which ushered in the literary Radicals of the 1930's.

Whitcombe and Tombs had a number of categories with which they defined their ratio of financial involvement in any given project. Much of the poetry they printed was paid for by the poet. If they felt that the product was inferior they would distance themselves with a disclaimer. If a title page had on it 'Printed for the author by Whitcombe and Tombs' it meant that the company took no responsibility for sales, distribution and so on.

One such publication heralded the new age of publishing, because its author soon linked with other young rebellious characters in the literary world to challenge the status quo which Whitcombe and Tombs had come to represent. *The Beggar* by R.A.K. Mason had no imprint at all, but a discreet notice on the back page to the effect that it had been printed at Whitcombe and Tombs. It was this attitude which led the author to get together with other poets and writers to make their own publications, so that Mason's book can be seen, both literally and figuratively, as a bridge between the old and the new.

There was very little outlet for books of literary endeavour during the pre-1930's period, although McEldowney in his essay in the *Oxford History of New Zealand Literature* does list a whole raft of publications such as student magazines, daily and weekly newspapers. Even monthlies like the *New Zealand Railways Magazine* had special supplements and space set aside for literary and poetic works. It makes the ex-newspaper man Curnow's idea "that 'almost nothing that matters was added to New Zealand's verse between 1906 and 1930'"[20] seem rather churlish. He and many others would build the basis for the first real literary "establishment" in New Zealand from the 1930's only because more adventurous presses began to appear which were willing to publish them. The 'revolution' of the 1930's had begun.

It was a heady mixture of left-wing politics and progressive attitudes towards literature and typography which heralded the arrival of the two major figures in the "revolution", Bob Lowry and Denis Glover. Working from different ends of the country, the former in Auckland, the latter in Christchurch, they revolutionized the way New Zealand viewed its literature by transforming the way writers were published.

Bob Lowry founded a press at the Auckland University College Student's Association in 1932 while working on the newly launched literary journal, **Phoenix**. Not long after he joined forces with R.A.K. Mason and Ron Holloway with the introduction of his own Unicorn Press. Under this imprint some early and influential titles were printed, probably the most significant of which was a small pamphlet entitled ***Conversations With my Uncle*** by a young writer called Frank Sargeson, published in 1936. Holloway, who had begun his own Griffin Press in 1934, soon took over Lowry's imprint. Lowry was a restless and unpredictable man and before his untimely suicide in 1963 he had begun and moved on from several other projects, most notably Pelorus Press and the Pilgrim Press, when again he joined forces with Ron Holloway.

Denis Glover, founder of the Caxton Press, was also a major catalyst for change in the publishing scene of the 1930's. Again the impetus came out of a university group with which James Bertram, Ian Milner and Charles Brasch were associated. Glover was not of the modern school as Lowry was, but he did acknowledge his influence and inspiration when he said of him, "if typography is a word that now some of us understand, the credit is Bob Lowry's."[21] For not only were this new crop of "revolutionaries" interested in what they published, they were also very concerned with their craft of printing and how things were published.

Having put out a few small volumes in the form of a small anthology entitled **New Poems**, a book of Glover's own work **Thistledown**, and **Three Poems** by Allen Curnow (who would have a long association with Glover over a forty year period as a friend and an author) the Caxton Press effectively came into being in 1936. Leo Bensemann joined Caxton in 1937. Trained in fine arts he brought the artist's eye to the book production of the press.

Later he was to become editor of **Landfall,** which under Charles Brasch became the premier arbiter of literary taste and style for a generation.

Like Lowry, Glover was a restless character and in a much celebrated part of his life he returned to the sea (he had been a sailor during the war), where he sailed with Albion Wright who was later to establish Pegasus Press.

It will be seen later on how this intermixing and mingling of personalities and identities is mirrored in the publishers and writers of the next "revolutionary" phase of New Zealand literature which began in the late 1960's and early 1970's through to the present day. This cross-pollination of ideas and productions is graphically represented in the bibliographies and questionnaires of the sample of publishers from the period 1969 to 1999 which I have gathered together as an adjunct to this thesis, and shows the fluidity and experimentation that took place both by writers and publishers who emerged out of the 60's generation.

I have concentrated on Glover and Lowry because the history of small press publishing is the story of the vision and initiative of individuals who are frustrated with the status quo at the time and who want to change the way things are done. The fact that both periods I have spoken about, 1830 to 1930 and 1930 to 1970, break into two sub-groups (1830 to 1880 then 1880 to 1930), and (1930 to 1945 then 1945 to 1969) is also significant. Both overall periods were broken up by war – the Land Wars in the case of the former, the Second World War in the case of the latter. The first phase of both eras can be seen as experimental, pushing the boundaries of ideas and methods of printing and publishing, while the second phase can be described as conservative and consolidatory.

After the end of World War II there was a push by Government and other sections of society to establish New Zealand as an homogenous nation. The years of depression and war meant that most people longed for a sense of stability and harmony. The notion of state patronage for writers and publishers was being talked about again, there having been a limited introduction of such things as literary grants during the pre-war years of the first Labour Government.

E.H. McCormick expressed the reservation that such patronage might lead to the encouragement of "the safe and second-rate,"[22] an argument, ironically now being aimed at the present-day, market-forces publishers. This sentiment was further expressed by A.R.D Fairburn, a fervent opponent to state patronage, who spoke about mushrooms growing out in the open while toadstools grew under trees. Others pointed to the arts under the Nazi and Soviet regimes as extreme examples of what can happen to state-funded writers.

While Caxton became the main literary publisher in the country, A.H. and A.W. Reed were the pre-eminent popular publishers of the post-war period. By the mid-fifties Caxton had introduced a whole new crop of writers including Smithyman, Sinclaire, Dallas and Frame. Earlier they had produced James K. Baxter's first book of poetry, Curnow's *A Book of New Zealand Verse*, and Sargeson's *When the Wind Blows*. An interesting ironic statement on the vagaries of publishers' choice of books can be seen when considering the fact that when Reed was publishing the well known drinker Barry Crump's best selling books, they could also decline publication of a book in the early seventies entitled *A Book on New Zealand Winemaking*. When questioned about this rejection A.H. Reed, a notorious teetotaler, replied "It's about alcohol isn't it?"

By the 1960's another major new player came on the scene under the imprint of Paul's Book Arcade. Blackwood and Janet Paul began to replace Caxton as the leading literary publishers in the country. They could also see the lack of published Māori writing as being significant and set about publishing *No Ordinary Sun* by Hone Tuwhare, begun by Bob Lowry and later taken over by Ron Holloway and Robin Lowry. Continuing along with this philosophy the Pauls "eventually made a name for encouraging Māori and Polynesian writers, including Patricia Grace and Albert Wendt."[23] Up to this point the only publication to specifically target Māori writers was *Te Ao Hou*, which had been instigated in the early 1950's by the Māori Affairs Department.

While it did introduce people such as Rowley Habib and Witi Ihimaera it never really gained acceptance in the Māori world, although during its existence it was certainly seen as an important literary magazine.[24]

However, with so much publishing being done by these larger presses and the cost of printing and publishing being out of the reach of many during this period, the small press industry began to become somewhat marginalised. Before his death Lowry published two of his most famous books, ***How to Ride a Bicycle in Seventeen Lovely Colours*** by Fairburn, and D'Arcy Cresswell's ***The Forest***. Glover moved to Wellington and worked for a while with Harry Tombs' Wingfield Press, who in some respects began the new wave of radical publishing in the 1930's with his production of ***Art in New Zealand*** and his own short-lived literary magazine, ***Rata***. And in the early sixties Glover began publishing again under Catspaw Press as well as several other imprints. There were also some other amateur presses working such as Mervyn Taylor's Mermaid, Louis Johnson's Capricorn, and Noel Haggard's Handcraft.

In addition, poets like R.A.K. Mason had become adept at the exploitation of small presses.[25] As an editor of literary and political journals, and an erstwhile partner to Lowry, Mason was familiar with the ins and outs of small press publication. With Fairburn and Geoffrey de Montalk he was part of a talented and eccentric trio in the New Zealand literary scene, in effect, a fore-runner of the type of person who would dominate the arena from the late sixties onwards.

But, however much the 'radicals' of the thirties still saw themselves in that vein, they had become by the end of the 1960's the literary 'establishment' of New Zealand. The fact that, except for Janet Paul, the main publishers of that time were male, Pakeha and becoming increasingly conservative in relation to the sixties generation now growing up around them, meant that they were beginning to lose their relevance.

Changes in technology also meant that small publishers no longer had to rely on printing expertise to put out a book. Photocopying and other forms of cheap reproduction enabled anybody who had written a poem to publish it. Another significant factor was the fact that much of the sixties publishing in New Zealand began to be overshadowed by large overseas publishers setting up shop here, like Collins and Heinemann, which had the effect of further marginalising un-economic projects, like poetry, from the mainstream.[26]

There was also the influence of the American Beat Generation and the European and New York avant-garde which transformed the intellectual climate. With the anti-establishment pop and counter-culture of the sixties, and the rising protest movement which focused on the Vietnam War, sexual and racial freedom and equal rights, a new generation was rising which saw how small presses and the printed word could facilitate their own end. To quote from **Book & Print in NZ**, "The 1970's saw a return to private presses by a generation that felt excluded from mainstream publication."[27]

For this survey footnotes have been kept to a minimum. Details of standard events (names, places, dates etc.) in printing and publishing history can be found in Bagnall, Andersen, Coleridge and Cave, Griffith, Robinson and Wattie, Sturm, and Williams, listed in the bibliography.

---

1. 'Bookmarks', **New Zealand Listener**, (5 March, 1990), p 129.
2. Johannes Andersen, 'Early Printing in New Zealand', **History of Printing in New Zealand** (Wellington:Wellington Club of Printing House Craftsmen, 1940), p 2.
3. Alan Loney, telephone interview with Michael O'Leary, 16.4.2000 (MA notebook).
4. Roderick Cave, **Private Presses**, 2nd ed. 1983, cited in **Book & Print in New Zealand** (Wellington: Victoria University Press, 1997), p 82.
5. **A Library Exhibition of Small Presses** (Wellington: NZ Book Council, 1977), p 2.

6. ***Oxford History of New Zealand Literature,*** 2nd ed. (Auckland: Oxford University Press, 1998), p 633.

7. Roderick Cave, ***Private Presses,*** 2nd ed. cited in ***Oxford History NZ Lit.,*** 2nd ed. p 633. Bagnall, in the ***New Zealand National Bibliography to 1889,*** p 396, listed 300 subscribers - a prophetic number in relation to the market for NZ poetry!

8. ***Oxford History of NZ Lit.,*** 2nd ed. p 635.

9. ***A Library Exhibition of Small Presses,*** p 3.

10. ***Oxford History NZ Lit.***, 2nd ed. p 632.

11. Bill Dacker, telephone interview with Michael O'Leary, 11.1.2000 (MA notebook).

12. Bill Dacker, ***Te Mamae me te Aroha*** (Dunedin: University of Otago Press, in association with the Dunedin City Council, 1994), p 68.

13. ***Oxford Companion to New Zealand Literature*** (Melbourne: Oxford University Press, 1998), p 516.

14. ***Oxford History of NZ Lit.,*** 2nd ed. p 633.

15. ***Oxford History of NZ Lit.,*** 2nd ed. p 636.

16. ***Oxford History of NZ Lit.,*** 2nd ed. p 636.

17. T.M. Hocken, ***A Bibliography of the Literature Relating to New Zealand,*** cited in Iris M. Park, ***New Zealand Periodicals of Literary Interest,*** (Wellington: Library School, National Library Service, 1962), p 1.

18. ***Oxford History of NZ Lit.,*** 2nd ed. p 634.

19. ***Oxford History of NZ Lit.,*** 2nd ed. p 642.

20. Allen Curnow, ***Look Back Harder, Critical Writings 1935 - 1984***, 1987, cited in ***Oxford History NZ Lit.,*** p 643.

21. ***A Library Exhibition of Small Presses,*** p 4.

22. ***Oxford History of NZ Lit.,*** 2nd ed., p 659.

23. ***Oxford History of NZ Lit.,*** 2nd ed., p 674.

24. ***Oxford History of NZ Lit.,*** 2nd ed., p 669.

25. ***A Library Exhibition of Small Presses,*** p 6.

26. ***Oxford History of NZ Lit.***, 2nd ed., p 672.

27. ***Book & Print in NZ,*** p 84.

Chapter Two

BUT IF YOU GO PUBLISHING PICTURES OF CHAIRMAN MAO...

In this chapter the discussion will focus on why the publishers who answered the questionnaire (and a few others who fit in to the overall context of this thesis) became involved in small press publishing. It will also look at the longevity or otherwise of the small press publishers, why some lasted longer than others and the reasons for success or failure. It will investigate some of the more significant publications and achievements of the individual small presses, how they relate to the overall picture of small press publishing in this country from 1969 to the present day and how it was influenced by the cultural 'revolution' of the sixties.

Worldwide, literary publishing is notoriously difficult to justify financially, and in a small market like New Zealand it is almost impossible to imagine someone going into this area to make a profit or to break even on a publishing enterprise. So what motivates people to become small press publishers. As Voice Press founder Lindsay Rabbitt comments "It didn't do anything for my finances."[1] He seems to be saying in a minimalist fashion what the majority of respondents imply.

In his recent introductory essay to the *Big Smoke* anthology, entitled *Poetics of the Impossible*, poet, actor and academic Murray

Edmond stated that "An enormous energy had been gathering itself together over the decade 1959 - 1969,"[2] especially in the poetry realm of the New Zealand literary scene. Edmond goes on to acknowledge something particularly pertinent to this present thesis by stating that "The poets included in **Big Smoke** produced 62 individual books of poems and broadsheets in the 16 years the collection spans, but 43 of these were published in the last five years, between 1971 and 1975."[3]

Analyzing these figures further Edmond states that of the 43 items listed as being published in the five year period to 1975, "Kevin Cunningham and Bill Manhire's Amphedesma Press and Trevor Reeves' Caveman Press together account for nearly half the books."[4] In fact, looking even closer at this comparison reveals an important and significant detail. Between 1970 and 1975 Amphedesma Press published eight books, the total number of titles they would ever publish. In the same period Caveman Press published 29 titles, and would go on publishing into the 1980's.

Thus, at the very beginning of the period this thesis covers we have two examples of the extreme positions which small press publishers represent in New Zealand. On the one hand Amphedesma was an attempt to publish writers who were 'new' to the literary scene but who Cunningham and Manhire recognised had talent, and therefore wanted to see in print. As Manhire puts it "I think we all wanted to be publishers back in the late 60's"[5] which backs up Murray Edmond's 'something in the air' feeling about the period. It was a "coy fantasy-world way of being a publisher"[6] Manhire admits, quite unlike the kind of operation Reeves got himself into.

Whereas Manhire used print-shop technology to have his print-ready material processed for Amphedesma, Reeves actually became a hands-on printer himself, having been donated a letter-press machine from Whitcoulls. Again, here at the outset of the period which this study covers, these two publishers provide a classic example of two extremes of the way in which the various players in this era went about small press publishing. As this period coincides with world-wide changes in printing technology, so a comparison between Caveman and Amphedesma gives a picture of how these two New Zealand publishers were able to take advantage of those changes: the former benefiting from a large local commercial enterprise getting rid of out-dated equipment, the latter making full use of the new cheap print shops available to them because they happened to be in London at the time.

The ultimate destiny of these two publishers is also of metaphorical significance in that they both represent the opposite ends of the spectrum in relation to acceptance by the literary establishment in New Zealand, and therefore act as a metaphor for the various positions the other publishers in this survey occupy in relation to that establishment. Bill Manhire's literary career has been well documented over the years and therefore Amphedesma Press, despite its rather small output, has a high profile in the annals of small press publishing in this country. On the other hand Caveman Press has felt itself relatively neglected by the "establishment", despite the impressive publication and author list they can claim.

This perception of unequal treatment, and the discrepancy created by it, is the main driving force behind this study. It is hoped that by providing bibliographical and factual evidence from questionnaire replies, that this situation will be redressed to some degree, or at least better understood. Trevor Reeves states the case for himself and other small presses in question nine of the questionnaire. "At one stage Caveman Press in the mid 1970's was publishing half the total books of poetry published in New Zealand. With other publishers of the time, mostly young, we were up to the three quarters mark, I estimate."

Trevor Reeves' impression of the powers that be in New Zealand literature finds focus in a publication like the ***Oxford Companion to New Zealand Literature:*** "A whole chunk of writers and publishers from the early to mid 1970's and even later, were omitted, including myself and Caveman Press."[7] If this is the case, it does seem extraordinary when one looks at Caveman's bibliography[8] Rightly or wrongly it illustrates the fact that some participants in the New Zealand publishing fraternity believe a gap exists between 'academic - establishment' literature and other groups in New Zealand writing and publishing.

Through the two publishers discussed in this chapter who represent two extreme positions (the establishment and the outsiders), it may be seen that over the last thirty years of small press publishing in New Zealand we have seen a division occur, one which is seen by some of the protagonists as significant and of an irreconcilable nature. To understand this phenomenon it is useful to discover why each person involved began publishing in the first place, what they hoped to achieve and to look at the longevity of each venture, why some continued and why others fell by the wayside. And why in a small country like ours such a divide has developed, one which has left many feeling cut-off, resentful and disaffected.

At the time most of the publishers in this survey began their careers they could have been almost universally considered non-conformist and to some degree anti-establishment. This was as true for Amphedesma as it was for Caveman, in that both saw that there were poets and writers who were not being published by mainstream publishers whom they felt should have their works in print. Indeed, Manhire mentions going to literary evenings in Dunedin in the early 70's at which "Trevor Reeves, who had started Caveman Press", was also in attendance.[9] This highlights one further aspect of New Zealand literature of the period, that is the interaction of many of the main players with each other.

In fact, many of the publishers in this study have collaborated with each other at various stages throughout the thirty years covered. Also, many of the writers and poets of the period have been published by more than one of the publishers mentioned. (See Table 4 and Table 5) Another aspect that this study observes is that some of the publishers have even published each other's work, for instance Caveman Press publishing Alan Loney, E.S.A.W. publishing Greg O'Brien, Hawk Press publishing Bill Manhire, Sudden Valley Press publishing Mark Pirie; throughout the bibliographies many other examples occur.

The pop culture revolution of the 1960's was a significant influence for one group of small publishers. In literary terms the trend was more influenced by the Beat Generation of 1950's America but energy of the early 70's was still very much that of the Beatles and the Rolling Stones and their inspiration to ordinary working-class kids, saying to them you don't have to put up with what *they* want you to do! As Bob Anderson recently wrote in an essay on The Bottle Press (which between 1969 and 1971 involved a collaboration between poet Sam Hunt and artist Robin White, among others including James K. Baxter) saying their focus was on "writing and publishing poems about things young people were interested in - love, booze, drugs, music."[10]

Peter Olds, who set up Montgomery Press to publish his own broadsheets and a book by Dunedin poet John Gibb, is one of the writers most closely associated with the marriage of literature and rock and roll. The ***Oxford Companion to New Zealand Literature*** cites Olds' "experience with music, drugs and the concerns and language of the streets"[11] as main motivations behind his writings. Also mentioned are Jack London, Allen Ginsberg, Jack Kerouac and the American music of the 1950's. The ***Companion*** finishes by speaking of Olds' later works in terms of "hallucinatory collage, but music remains a strong influence, with references made to Tom Waits and John Lennon."[12] Olds himself speaks of his experience as a publisher in music terminology, likening the publication of a new broadsheet to a band releasing a rpm 45 single record, while the analogy is made to a book being the equivalent of an album being released.[13]

This connection between the music of the sixties and New Zealand publishing continues through the 1970's. As Alan Brunton states one of the main influences in his decision to be a publisher was the example of The Beatles setting up Apple Records.[14]

Brunton saw the appeal of this as artists having control over their own works, another major reason behind many of the publishing ventures of the past three decades. And just as the Beatles had pioneered the idea of the artist writing their own songs in the early sixties, so the notion that writers and poets could publish their own work began to permeate the small press industry to the extent that by the end of the 1980's the majority of small press publishers in New Zealand were writers themselves.

David Eggleton also set up his own press for exactly the same reason, to have control over his own writing "in order not to have to structure my poetry according to the formats of the mainstream literary magazines in the late seventies."[15] While Eggleton in recent times has become well-known as a Polynesian poet, he acknowledges his debt to the back cover raves of early Bob Dylan albums as having an influence on his decision to become a writer and a publisher. This is another tangible example of New Zealand publishing being directly influenced by the music of the sixties. However, the youthful ideology of the sixties was beginning to wane, particularly with the murder of John Lennon. I attempted to convey the sense of deepening scepticism in the title and the sentiment of **The Flipside of the Ballad of John and Yoko,** a poem in which the unequivocal line "Fuck the revolution, we have bred another generation"[16] summed up for me what seemed to be the spirit of the times.

Bob Dylan himself had been influenced by the American 1950's Beat Generation poets such as Ginsberg and Lawrence Ferlinghetti. The Beat Movement is described as being a revolution of "experimental forms, metaphysical content, and provocative anti-intellectual, anti-hierarchical spirit of the movement spread across America and then beyond the English-speaking world, to be taken up by second and third generation writers (Yevtushenko, Voznesensky, Bob Dylan, the Beatles, Wolf Biermann), evolving a 'counter-culture' which had a widespread and in many ways lasting impact."[17] Looking at that list of 'serious writers' and 'pop icons' illustrates how much a part of literary convention both have become.

The next grouping of seventies publishers are those who could be termed 'literary' publishers. Their main interest in producing literature involved the marriage of high quality printing and aesthetic presentation with what they considered the best of their generation's literary output. They too had been influenced by the American literature of the fifties and sixties, but by the more intellectual and avant-garde end of the spectrum, rather than the popular culture figures already discussed. One important publication at the time of the early 1970's was the anthology edited by Arthur Baysting, ***The Young New Zealand Poets,*** which included many of the people who are the focus of this part of the present thesis; Alan Brunton, Sam Hunt, Alan Loney, Bill Manhire, Bob Orr etc. The debt to the sixties is acknowledged later on in the eighties and nineties by Brunton (***Years ago Today***) and one of Loney's authors, Wystan Curnow (***Back in the USA***).

An important difference between this group of young writers and publishers and the 'radicals' of the 1930's, was that the focus and literary inspiration came from international sources, rather than the inward-looking earlier generation who had tried to establish a 'New Zealand' literature free of external influence. This mixture of pop culture, literature, avant-garde art and performance is perhaps best represented by Alan Brunton and the Red Mole group who did the majority of their work in New York, but always kept their New Zealand identity. They in turn may well have taken their name from the English radical magazine, ***Red Mole***, which had an association with that most extreme duo of intellectual, artistic, political, drugged, musical, radical pastiche, John Lennon and Yoko Ono.[18]

Those represented in Baysting's anthology were basically the ***FREED*** group, and despite what Alan Loney asserts in his answer to the questionnaire, that this group's achievements have not been acknowledged even today,[19] the fact is that if one looks at the names represented it is obvious that one is confronted with the 'new establishment' of the New Zealand literary world, thirty years after they burst on the scene as the 'new poets'!

The ubiquitous and somewhat enigmatic figure of Loney himself is prominent in small press publishing in this country from the mid-seventies. With his Hawk Press he became in a sense the successor to Amphedesma Press, and indeed, four of the seven poets published by Manhire and Cunningham appear on the Hawk Press bibliography. Also, the last Amphedesma title appears in 1975, the same year as the first Hawk Press publication. While Loney is a hands-on craftsman when it comes to book production, philosophically, aesthetically and to a large extent in literary taste, both Hawk and Amphedesma share a much closer affinity than the other more egalitarian or populist small presses of the era.

One of the major influences behind the scenes in New Zealand literature in the early seventies was the American poetry exemplified by the Black Mountain poets. To a large extent this was a result of the influence of people like Wystan Curnow and Roger Horrocks, both of whom were poets and academics at Auckland University at the time where they established their ground-breaking papers in American Literature. A more tangible and direct connection with small presses in New Zealand and the Black Mountain poets is when one of their number, Robert Creeley, came to New Zealand in 1976, Hawk Press published a book of his poetry, **Hello.**[20]

Another direct connection with Hawk Press and American literature is the collaboration with Brick Row Publishers in the publication of Roger Horrocks' book **Auckland Regional Transit Poetry Line** in 1982.[21] One of Brick Row's main contributions to the small press fraternity was their distribution network, which is sorely missed since their return to the United States. Oz and Ruth Kraus of Brick Row were both New Yorkers originally and a significant non-New Zealand publisher they distributed in this country was the influential American imprint, Black Sparrow Press.

Indeed, some local publishers, myself among them, were influenced by the style evoked by them to the point that they incorporated aspects of the Americans in their own designs. For example, Michael Gifkins writing in the **Listener** in 1990, more than a decade after Hawk Press published Creeley's book, remarked that one of the books published by my own press, the Earl of Seacliff Art Workshop, was "virtually indistinguishable in its non-laminated soft covers and elegant end-papers from the adventurous American West Coast imprint Black Sparrow Press."[22]

This embracing of American culture by the 'radical' generation of new publishers and writers which grew out of the sixties and their predecessors is in direct contrast to the 'radicals' of the thirties and forties who expressed their radicalism by rejecting overseas influence, particularly that of the British Edwardian literary tradition, which they considered at the time to be stifling the development of a true 'New Zealand' literature. Indeed, a debate continues throughout the seventies, the eighties and on into the final decade of the twentieth century over what exactly New Zealand small presses should publish. Many, through the questionnaire, express a desire to break out of a perceived narrow and parochial New Zealand literary scene, and some even cite this as a reason for their involvement in publishing in the first place.

There was a perception among small press publishers of a widening gap between those who were seen as 'establishment' and those who published a more alternative list. This became the catalyst for offering an alternative to mainstream and commercial publishers who appeared to have lost touch with what the new generation of writers and poets were expressing, or who simply had no desire to publish books which wouldn't make a profit.

The bibliographies suggest that through the far-sightedness and hard work of many of the small presses a lot of now well known authors got their initial start. Alister Taylor, for example, published Tim Shadbolt's ***Bullshit and Jellybeans,*** along with writer, publisher and home brewer Malcolm Gramaphone's prophetic classic, ***The Brewer's Bible.*** Taylor was also responsible for two of the more controversial books of the earlier period of this study, ***The Little Red Schoolbook*** and the infamous ***James K. Baxter, 1926 - 1972: a memorial volume.***[23]

As the 1970's progressed small presses began to proliferate throughout New Zealand , many more than can be covered in an introductory study such as the present one. However, it is hoped that this will act as a catalyst to further study and understanding of the unique and important contribution which these publishers have made to the survival and furthering of literature in New Zealand. The bibliographies of those twenty three publishers who answered the questionnaire, plus a few additional bibliographies which fill in the picture more fully, show the extent and the interconnectedness of these small press publishers from 1969 to 2000, (See Table 4).

Despite obvious differences, an underlying unifying factor is a desire by small press publishers to see in print works of literature and other writings which had little or no hope of being published elsewhere, many of which through the passage of time have more than proven their worth, some even becoming New Zealand classics. Many of the publishers were writers who wanted to see their own and other's works published as they saw fit. By the last couple of years of the decade Lindsay Rabbitt's Voice Press had appeared, publishing among others early works of Chris Else and Mike Johnson. He also produced works by Bob Orr, Geoff Cochrane, L.E. Scott and an early appearance by Apirana Taylor.

Caveman Press continued expanding their impressive list of titles and authors throughout the seventies and into the eighties, with such notable authors as Hone Tuwhare, Peter Olds, James K. Baxter, Murray Edmond, Dennis List, David Mitchell, Alan Loney and Rachel McAlpine. A notable first for this press was the anthology of New Zealand women's poetry published in 1977, **Private Gardens,** edited by Riemke Ensing. Another publisher who covers similar ground over a similar time frame as Reeves was Barry Mitcalfe and his Coromandel Press.[24] Among those published by Mitcalfe are Ron Riddell, Gary Mutton and Haare Williams. Mitcalfe's own significant book **Maori** is among the list of titles and his book of poetry, **Migrant** was published by Caveman in 1975.

A distinctive feature of small press publishing in New Zealand over the last thirty years has been the close relationship between the printed word and the use of visual images in the presentation of literary works. From the early publications of Amphedesma Press using a Ralph Hotere drawing for the cover of Bob Orr's book, and a different Hotere illustration for one of Manhire's own volumes, artists and writers have collaborated together on many projects.

As the eighties approached one of the new publishers on the scene, Chris Moisa with his One-Eyed Press, was himself a visual artist as well as a poet. He had actually begun publishing first in 1973 with the poetry book **Abecedary** written by Mark Williams, who went on to become a well respected literary critic and academic. As the seventies merged into the eighties Moisa developed a distinctive publishing style which included illustration as well as words, most of the artwork by himself, as in the case of his publications by Iain Sharp and Peter Olds, although on one of his projects Otago artist Robin Swanney-MacPherson did the honours.

This marriage of art and literature has meant that many of the country's notable artistic talents have participated in small press productions. These include Michael Illingworth, Nigel Brown, Janet Paul, Andrew Drummond, Roy Dalgarno, Kathryn Madill and Robin White. One person who has embraced all three aspects, artwork, writing and publishing, is the prolific Gregory O'Brien. O'Brien began his small press publishing career in the mid- eighties with his imprint, Miracle Mart Receiving. Other O'Brien publishing incarnations emerged throughout the eighties and into the nineties, including Modern House, Wellington Plains, Keretene Press and Animated Figure. He is still active today in all three fields and as well as illustrating his own works has done artwork for other writers, including Elizabeth Smither.

The 1980's saw the emergence of small publishers who were dedicated to specific kinds of literary issues and to a certain extent became a decade of consolidation, following on from the 'revolutionary' fervour of the 1970's. By the first few years of the eighties most of those who were prominent in the seventies had moved on to other careers (where money could be attained) or had taken on a different manifestation. The new concerns of the decade became issues such as feminism, which was taken up by poet Heather McPherson, who saw a whole generation of talented women writers and artists unable to get their work published or exhibited.

The Spiral Collective, and later on Wendy Harrex's New Women's Press[25] redressed the situation by setting up publishing houses to encourage women as writers who couldn't get their works published in the then male dominated arena. The women's liberation movement of the seventies was the catalyst for these women to become publishers in the eighties.

Another 'issues' publisher who began putting out books in the early eighties was Bernard Gadd of Hallard Press. As a secondary school teacher in South Auckland he noticed a lack of books and other literature which had any interest or relevance to his mainly Māori and Polynesian students. This coupled with his interest in left-wing politics led him to begin writing stories which he could read to his pupils, who generally came from working-class homes. He also encouraged others to write by setting up two further publishing enterprises, Hillary Press and Te Ropu Kahurangi, to specifically encourage his students and workmates.

Meanwhile, Hallard Press was publishing poetry and other works of literature. The biggest venture they undertook was the publication of the novel ***Kaspar's Journey*** by the author of the New Zealand classic war novel ***A Soldier's Tale,*** M.K. Joseph. This was a joint project with another small press, Brick Row Publishing, who were getting a reputation in their own right for being the foremost distributors for books published by New Zealand small presses. Indeed, they were the only people to tackle this major problem which all New Zealand small publishing enterprises face in a country with a small population scattered throughout two long islands with difficult terrain. As Bernard Gadd laments about the decision of Oz and Ruth Kraus to return to the United States, "No-one has replaced Brick Row, and I miss their services."[26]

Apart from the political focus of Heather McPherson and her interest in women's rights and homosexual law reform, and people like Niel Wright and Bernard Gadd with their overtly left-wing outlook, the small presses which developed throughout the eighties were dedicated to publishing books of a more literary nature. The majority of small presses prominent in the 1970's had , by the mid-1980's fallen by the wayside, (See Table 2) although individuals from those presses such as Reeves, Brunton and Manhire continued to be involved in different manifestations.

Bill Manhire asserts in his questionnaire that he is relatively unknown as a publisher (outside the rarefied air that was Amphedesma) but ironically this is possibly where one of his major achievements lies, as much as his teaching or writing. As he puts it, "Probably the thing I'm least known for, but where you might say my influence has been fairly extensive, is my work over the last twenty years for Victoria University Press."[27] This is significant as many of the university presses now undertake a good deal more literary publishing than before, and in some respects have usurped the traditional areas of small press publishers in the last decade or so.

Among the newcomers of the 'literary' small presses to emerge from the early to mid-eighties were Donald Kerr's Prometheus Press, my own E.S.A.W., John Denny's Puriri Press, and Black Robin Press which began as a joint venture between its founder, Bill Wieben and Alan Loney. Loney then went on to form another press entitled Black Light Press in the late 1980's which published among other titles Wystan Curnow's book of poetry ***Back in the USA***, a title which echoes the Beatles 1968 satirical song ***Back in the USSR***, which shows that even twenty years later the sixties were still a potent force in the background of cultural iconography, even in the high-brow conceptual world of post-modernism.

Almost a decade forward from Curnow's book Alan Brunton and his Bumper Books imprint would publish in 1998 his own book of 'language and performance' of that era entitled ***Years Ago Today***, another direct evocation of a Beatles classic from 1967, ***Sergeant Pepper's Lonely Hearts Club Band,*** a song which began with the words "It was twenty years ago today / Sergeant Pepper taught the band to play."[28] Even Nag's Head Press published poetry by rock singer Bill Direen.

Throughout the 1980's Warwick Jordan's Hard Echo Press was both prolific and successful in putting out a number of early publications by writers who would go on to become well known and taken up by larger publishers. Despite this Jordan comes out of the exercise embittered and almost bankrupted, both financially and in terms of his personal energy. His tone is probably best summed up in his final statement to the questionnaire for this survey in which he states "In the modern day literary scene I helped a number of now established writers - authors (e.g. Rosie Scott, Mike Johnson, Stephanie Johnson, James Norcliffe, Iain Sharp). Most of them are mentioned in the various literary surveys (***Oxford History of New Zealand Literature*** etc.) I'm not"[29]

This is not quite true. Noel Waite in his essay on 'Private printing' in ***Book & Print in New Zealand*** displayed admiration for Jordan's Hard Echo which he acknowledged "achieved the feat of hand-setting an entire novel, Mike Johnson's *Lear* (1986)."[30] However, Jordan's disaffection and alienation from the literary mainstream in New Zealand, which is shared with many others including Gadd, Reeves, Moisa, and even Loney and to a certain extent Brunton, does suggest that a rift between the 'individuals' and the perceived establishment, which began in the seventies, has widened.

One of the more innovative but commercially disappointing publications by Hard Echo Press was a two book and cassette publication in 1985 called *The Globe Tapes,* edited by Rosemary Menzies. This featured 42 poets who had appeared at readings organized by poet David Mitchell at the Globe Tavern throughout the 1980's. Mitchell, whose ground-breaking volume of poetry *Pipe Dreams in Ponsonby* had first been published in 1971 by Stephen Chan, with a re-print the following year by Caveman, was an inspiration to many poets and writers all through the 1980's. He, himself had been an innovative and experimental poet for many years "exhibiting 'open form' since the early sixties"[31] and *Pipe Dreams in Ponsonby* "elevated him to something of guru status among the emergent poets of the 1970's."[32]

This direct link which Mitchell provided with the sixties, seventies and eighties made him a significant person and his weekly readings at the Globe provided a regular focal point for writers and poets, not only for those in Auckland where they were held but throughout the country. Many of the poets began their own small press projects in order to have something to sell at poetry readings, in the same way that David Eggleton and Peter Olds had done before them. John Pule, Brian Gregory, Sandra Bell, Kim Blackburn and Ron Riddell along with many others published in this manner.

As the eighties and the nineties began to merge high hopes were held that small press publishing in New Zealand would become recognized as an important part of the overall publishing picture. An expression of this is stated by Michael Gifkins in his 'Bookmarks' column in the *Listener* at the beginning of the new decade, where he asserts that "Books from such presses as Nag's Head, Wai-te-Ata,

Hawk, Black Light, Griffin and (early) Caxton display an attention to typography and design that makes them benchmarks for the more alert of the commercial publishers . . . the lessons of the small presses are likely to be increasingly heeded by mainstream publishers."[33]

The early 1990's turned out to be a less than successful time for many small presses in New Zealand. To a certain extent they became victims of their own success, with the mainstream publishers heeding the lessons of small presses and becoming more mindful of the aesthetics of book production and other aspects of publishing normally associated with small presses. Also, none of the small presses could match the deals being offered some authors by big publishers even though their talents had been discovered and nurtured by the small presses in the first place. This was particularly difficult for the likes of Hard Echo.[34]

Another factor to have a significant impact on the viability of small presses in the world of literary publishing was the introduction to the market on a large scale of the university presses in the last decade or so. Having the resources of a major educational institution behind them, and with people of the stature, talent and influence of Bill Manhire in the case of Victoria, and Wendy Harrex for Otago University Press involved, both of whom had cut their teeth on the crusts of small press publishing, made for a winning combination.

Not that these new aspects have deterred small presses in New Zealand in the nineties. They continue to spring up at regular intervals, and the old brigade marches on in one form or another. The increase in interest in contemporary Māori and Polynesian writing, begun to a certain degree by Hallard Press, has developed more fully in the nineties, "Huia Publishers in 1991 led a move by Māori themselves into publishing. Pasifika Press (formerly Polynesian Press) continued to be the primary provider of Polynesian books"[35] and while these two are not primarily literary presses they are increasingly becoming the main publishers of new Māori and Pacific Island writers in New Zealand. An interesting note is that there was a previous but unrelated imprint called Huia Publishers, run by Tim

Shadbolt and Miriam Cameron when they lived at Huia Beach west of Auckland.

New small publishers of literature, both poetry and prose, have shown a commitment to putting out material that the more commercial enterprises won't undertake, a perennial function of small presses in this country over the past thirty years. Such people as Mark Pirie of HeadworX and John O'Connor of Sudden Valley Press are continuing this tradition. The bibliographies and questionnaire responses from small press publishers assembled in this document express the achievements and motivations of the protagonists very well, in other words they speak for themselves. It is obvious that the non-conformist aspect of the revolution of the sixties permeated through the small press movement and still has an influence today.

In some respects a new 'sixties' appears on the contemporary horizon, at least in terms of new technologies if not ideologies. As we move into the twenty-first century the small publishers are gearing up to accept new challenges. Computer technology, on-line publishing, CD-ROM and other neo-conventional forms of presenting literature are being explored by our small presses. Bumper Books and Banshee Productions delve into the area of literary video and film, with such productions as Sally Rodwell's study of poets Alan Brunton and Michelle Leggott, *Heaven's Cloudy Smile,* and Clare O'Leary's film about playwright Mervyn Thompson, *A Class Act*[36] along with her film *The Sound of a Painting: poetry - painting - film* which captured the exhibition curated by Gregory O'Brien of Ralph Hotere's work celebrated by many leading New Zealand writers.[37] Meanwhile many others still continue to produce innovative and uncompromising texts on printed paper. Also, the recent show organized by singer/songwriter Charlotte Yates, *Baxter,* a tribute by rock-stars and performers, including David Eggleton, to the poetry of James K. Baxter, shows a continuation of the merging of words and music from a new generation.

---

1. Questionnaire response - Voice Press, Q5, p182.

2. ***Big Smoke: New Zealand Poems 1960 - 1975*** (Auckland: Auckland University Press, 2000), p 29.
3. ***Big Smoke,*** p 30.
4. ***Big Smoke,*** p 30.
5. Questionnaire response - Amphedesma Press, Q1, p61.
6. Bill Manhire, ***Doubtful Sounds*** (Wellington: Victoria University Press, 2000), p 26.
7. Questionnaire response - Caveman Press, Q4, p85.
8. Questionnaire response - Caveman Press Bibliography, pp82, 83.
9. ***Doubtful Sounds,*** p 27.
10. ***Bottle Creek: Exhibition Booklet*** (Wellington: Porirua Museum of Arts and Cultures, 1998), p 4.
11. ***Oxford Companion to NZ Lit.,*** p 413.
12. ***Oxford Companion to NZ Lit.,*** p 413.
13. Questionnaire response - Montgomery Press, p125.
14. Questionnaire response - Bumper Books, Q2, p79.
15. Questionnaire response - Bard Press, p65.
16. Michael O'Leary, ***Flipside to the Ballad of John and Yoko*** (Auckland: E.S.A.W., 1980), p 2.
17. ***Oxford Companion to English Literature*** 5th ed., First TSP impression, (Oxford: Oxford University Press, 1996), p 77.
18. Jerry Hopkins, ***Yoko Ono: A biography*** (London: Sidgwick & Jackson, 1987), p 159.
19. Questionnaire response - Hawk Press, Q1, p108.
20. Questionnaire response - Hawk Press Bibliography, p106.
21. Questionnaire response - Hawk Press Bibliography, p106.
22. Michael Gifkins, 'Bookmarks', ***New Zealand Listener,*** 5 March 1990, p129.
23. Preliminary bibliography of Alister Taylor, pp193, 194.
24. Preliminary bibliography of Coromandel Press, pp185, 186.
25. Preliminary bibliography of New Womens Press, pp191, 192.
26. Questionnaire response - Hallard Press, Q6, p98.
27. Questionnaire response - Amphedesma Press, Q9, p63.
28. The Beatles, Back of Album Cover, ***Sergeant Pepper's Lonely Hearts Club Band*** (London: Parlophone Records, 1967), track 1.
29. Questionnaire response - Hard Echo Press, Q9, p105.
30. Noel Waite, 'Private printing', ***Book & Print in New Zealand: A Guide to Print Culture in Aotearoa*** (Wellington, Victoria University Press, 1997), p 82.
31. ***Oxford History of NZ Lit,*** 2nd ed. p 679.
32. ***Oxford Companion to NZ Lit.,*** p 378.
33. ***Listener***, 5 March, 1990, p129.
34. Questionnaire response - Hard Echo Press, Q8 & 9, p105.
35. ***Oxford History of NZ Lit.,*** 2nd ed. p 683.
36. Deborah Shepard, ***Reframing Women: a history of New Zealand film*** (Auckland: Harper Collins, 2000), p 166.
37. Gregory O'Brien, ***Hotere: out the black window, Ralph Hotere's work with New Zealand poets*** (Wellington: Godwit, in association with City Gallery, 1997).

Chapter Three

PRINTING, DISTRIBUTION AND ODIOUS COMPARISONS

This chapter concerns itself with the 'nuts and bolts' as it were of small press publishing, the way various of the publishers surveyed went about physically producing their books, whether through the hands-on involvement of those in the fraternity who had trained as printers, or those who contracted their work out to commercial printers. We will look more closely at the difficulties with distribution already alluded to, the problems of funding the various operations and how these impacted upon the longevity or otherwise of the presses. Also, it looks at the scene in New Zealand publishing in the 1970's and through statistical analysis shows how small presses fitted in to the situation and their impact, if any, on the overall publishing trends of the time. It will make some comparisons with similar situations encountered overseas, both in small press publishing and literary publishing generally and will look at the attitudes and realities of state and private funding philosophies through the presses themselves, and how they impacted upon the literary indigenous publishing in New Zealand. The individual responses to the questionnaire which follow provide an intimate insight into the behind the scenes, day to day running of a small press and are thus invaluable documentary evidence.

"Handsetting is a slow painstaking job that could not be farmed out easily, and before long it took its toll on Patric's eyesight."[1] While set up in the early 1960's to print programmes for Dunedin's Globe Theatre and thus only indirectly related to literary publishing, the effect of using handset type is well described here by Rosalie Carey and is probably a more honest assessment than might be forthcoming from an aficionado who may be more protective of the effects of their trade. But it makes more pertinent Noel Waite's admiration of Warwick Jordan's feat of handsetting an entire novel.[2]

Roughly a third (seven out of twenty three) of the small press publishers who answered the questionnaire claim to have used hand set printing to produce their books. The reasons for the use of such antiquated technology are as many and varied as the people themselves.

Warwick Jordan describes his first foray into handset printing as involving a bit of 'footsetting' as well. He explains "I taught myself how to print as I found printing too poor a quality or too expensive for my non-existent budget. I bought the gear and figured it out. *Tuatara* (HEP's first publication) was originally printed without a printing press (I just stood on it)", and Jordan then admits that "printing was a means to an end for me, I never produced anything of superior printing quality."[3] This utilitarian view is reiterated by Heather McPherson of the Spiral Collective who explains that despite the gratitude she felt to Alan Loney for his support she didn't enjoy working on "elderly printing presses . . . The physical work was tiring; I realized that the priority for me was not beautiful and/or old-style printing but getting the work out."[4]

At the other end of the scale are the exponents and advocates of the "elderly printing presses" who use their skill at printing on these old machines to produce books of aesthetic and lasting quality. One of the foremost practitioners of this technology is Alan Loney of Hawk Press who became involved in publishing initially because he felt "that books that were being published could be better designed and produced than was the case at the time."[5] Loney's expertise in the production of high quality book production through the use of "letterpress, with handset metal type, hand printing and hand sewing and binding"[6] and many of the titles from Hawk Press in particular have become sought after collectors items.

In fact this is the case with many of the productions of small presses in New Zealand over the last thirty years, including the longest running press surveyed by questionnaire for this thesis, Bob Gormack of Christchurch's Nag's Head Press, who "has long been noted for his impeccable printing and the special flavour of his writing"[7], and indeed many of Nag's Head earlier books now fetch good prices on the second hand book market.

The interest in small private press hand printing was prophetically predicted by Walter Lemm of Auckland's Imp Press, who in 1973 founded the Association of Handcraft Printers, now an established organisation with over seventy members. Noel Waite in his article on private printing states that a catalogue of the books belonging to the association "as of July 1993 was issued in 1993 by the Librarian, John Denny, from his Puriri Press, Auckland"[8] which shows how the association has grown and how influential and organized this aspect of small press publishing is in New Zealand.

However, for the majority of small press publishers the primary concern is to get the book out in some printed form because they want people to be able to read what the writer or poet has written. In the early 1970's the mood of the reading public was beginning to change. A wider definition of 'literature' began to emerge and this in turn affected the type of things publishers were prepared to put out. The 1975 International Women's Year saw an increasing demand for works by women writers, which was behind the emergence of the Spiral Collective, and later the New Women's Press. Māori writers also began to tell the stories of the tangata whenua in their own words more openly, yet a truly Māori small press would not emerge until the nineties with the advent of Huia Publishers. As Mark Williams observes in relation to the new readership of the 70's, "Just as important, perhaps, the economics of publishing were changing as a more substantial and differentiated market for New Zealand writing began to take shape."[9]

As well as the recycling of old machinery assisting the "economics of publishing" by small press publishers there was an increase in new technological developments which also facilitated the activities of such enterprises. Ironically, it was Mark Williams' own 1973 collection of poetry, **Abecedary**, which was to benefit from a new and cheap form of reproduction, that is a combination of photocopying plus off-set printing using paper plates in place of the traditional, more expensive metal ones.

Mark Williams' publisher, Chris Moisa of One-Eyed Press, puts it thus, "and that was the key word, cheap. It was very cheap to publish using a photocopier and more importantly you had total control over your own work."[10] It is these two elements, cost and editorial control, which dominate the minds of small press publishers throughout this study and which most of them keep returning to in answer to the questionnaire. Whether it is using previously acquired printing skills such as the likes of Lindsay Rabbitt with Voice Press, the recruitment of understanding commercial printers as in the case of E.S.A.W. and Prometheus Press whose Donald Kerr speaks of a "large bill with a friendly printer. The latter a most necessary thing"[11] or the use of the more recent developments in technology such as personal computer and printers which can be controlled from home, the search for a cheaper and better form of book production is the constant concern of small presses.

Within these broad goals many variations occur and because of the individualistic and often eccentric nature of many of the people involved in small press publishing there is a wide range of solutions. Now that print-runs can be tailored to suit individual books publishing large editions is no longer necessary. For example, Pemmican Press whose "printing is done on laser and inkjet printers attached to a PC"[12] have an average print-run of 100 copies of each edition.

With the general acceptance of "computer technology [which] allowed small runs, self-published, self distributed"[13] many people are now exploring 'on-line' publishing as eulogized by the likes of Trevor Reeves.[14] Conversely, Niel Wright of Original Books has a philosophy based on the importance of the text being preserved in hard copy, often only putting out three or four copies of an individual title and pays scant notice to the aesthetics of book production, although this leads to a kind of individualistic minimalism which creates a charm of its own. Gregory O'Brien often only produces a small number of copies of his hand-produced titles which give many of his books the feel of individually produced works of art.

"The simplest way to distribute a printed work is for an author to deliver his or her own work directly to the reader. This method has always been the favoured or desperate last resort of some."[15] Distribution has always been a major difficulty for small press publishers in New Zealand and as suggested in the above sentence whether "favoured or desperate last resort" the footslog method of book distribution has certainly been a reality for a number of the protagonists. Again Warwick Jordan puts the case unequivocally. "I tried professional distributors, but they weren't much help. Distribution was the big problem for a small press, a lot of it was door-knocking at shops run by morons."[16] Indeed, most of those who answered have done a variety of activities to distribute their books.

The only real attempt to tackle this aspect of small press publishing in any meaningful way was carried out by Oz and Ruth Kraus of Brick Row Publishing. By 1984 they had set up a distribution network to distribute their own publications and by the end of the 1980's were doing distribution for many other small presses throughout New Zealand, including Hawk Press, E.S.A.W., Hallard Press, Voice Press and Black Robin Press, on a commission basis.

Brick Row represented the only real attempt by a small publisher to come to grips with this difficult aspect of small press activity in this country.

However, many others have dealt with the problem of distribution in other ways. Some like Eggleton's Bard Press, Sandra Bell's Apron Press, Old's Montgomery Publications and Stephen Oliver's Horizontal Press were established so that their creators had available works to sell at poetry readings, a major form of distribution for many writers in New Zealand even today. And while the primary concern of this study is the printed word it is also important to remember other forms of distribution are available to many of the poets and writers mentioned in this thesis.

Thus the mixture of pop culture and new technology, as Mark Pirie observes citing Murray Edmond and Mary Paul's 1987 publication ***The New Poets: Initiatives in New Zealand Poetry,*** has meant poets such as Kim Eggleston, Cilla McQueen, Sam Hunt, L.E Scott, Gary McCormick (who began his career with a small press of his own, Piano Press), Bill Direen and David Eggleton can "reach a wide audience through either television appearances or via tape, video, CD, microphone, record and album."[17] All, in effect, alternative forms of distribution. Pirie himself chooses to publish through the conventional book form using his HeadworX imprint, for which his "books are distributed in New Zealand and Australia by reputable distributors."[18]

The length of time a small press remains in operation is often determined by the factors so far discussed in this chapter. Cost, distribution and lack of a large enough market to sustain an on-going publishing venture, are all aspects to be considered when assessing the longevity. Looking at who has survived and who has had to give it up (see Table 2), we can see that the ones who stayed on are those who take the least notice of practical realities, or else they are those who to a degree are able to make the rules fit in with them rather than be dictated by them.

Alan Brunton of Bumper Books expresses his disdain for "market forces" by proclaiming that as a publisher his "freedom lies in the fact that the market comes to us."[19] Original Book's Niel Wright gets around the problem of publishing in a capitalist environment by producing small print runs, or only producing single copies to fulfil individual orders. He also puts minimum emphasis on getting his titles known, instead "relying on the National Bibliography and other book data bases here and world wide to bring my publications to notice."[20]

It appears from statistics that small presses produce between 5% and 20% of the literary publications in New Zealand in any given year and that literary publishing in general produces between 5% and 10% of all printed and published works in the same period. (see

Table 3) While there are many variables in these calculations, both in the statistics and the factual data, the fact that small presses, while only contributing from .2% to .9% of total publishing, make up a sizeable contribution to the literary output in this country and have done consistently throughout the overall time covered by this study.

The late 1960's, early 1970's, saw a dramatic increase in book publishing throughout the western, English-speaking world. To a certain extent the flourishing of small, independent presses in this period is a mirror image of what was happening to literary book publishing generally. For example, in England between 1964 and 1978 the total publication of works of literature went from 556 titles to 805. A similar increase from 351 titles in 1964 to 583 in 1978 can be seen in publication of poetry volumes. A high point in both categories was reached in the late 60's, early 70's. For example, 932 works of literature were published in 1968, while poetry books reached their highest point in 1973 with a total of 771 titles published.[21]

The New Zealand situation was similar, although slightly behind the English

scene. For example, the leap in numbers does not occur until 1970 when literary publications rose from 59 the previous year, to almost double at 108. As with the English example which appears to taper off after its high point, the New Zealand figure seems to peak in 1978 with the publication of 178 literary titles before dropping back to between 130 and 150 in the early 1980's. (see Table 3) And between 1970 and 1978 there was a steady increase occurring which followed the English experience also, albeit a few years later.

One interesting point of departure between small press publishing and larger mainstream publishers is the fragmentation and energy-sapping division it engenders. Whereas the trend in the major publishing houses in England and around the world since World War Two meant that publishing "and subsequently bookselling, followed the national [English] and international pattern in becoming group-minded"[22] the small presses all remain fiercely individual. Alan Brunton probably best sums it up when he says,

"One does not count the cost - two might; that's why one must work alone."[23]

The experience in the United States is similar, although with peculiarities unique to the number one exponent of the capitalist corporate takeover. For example, Kilgour writes of a phenomenon "of the twentieth century [in publishing] occurring after the Second World War and almost entirely in the United States was the conglomerate merger, which had as its principal characteristic the acquisition of businesses whose activities were not related to those of the acquirer."[24] The significance of this is that books became a commodity like any other consumer item. To a certain extent small presses off-set this trend by not catering for a mass market and by seeing a book as something akin to an art work.

Giving a more complete picture of the American scene Kilgour does concede that as the twentieth century drew to a close he could see that "there are still many independent traditional publishers as well as more than fifty independent electronic-book publishers."[25] Thus the similarities between the contemporary US scene for small independent publishers and those who answered the questionnaires about the contemporary New Zealand situation are quite close except for the scale of operations and numbers involved. In a way the larger multi-national publishing houses may actually ensure the survival of the independents as writers and poets strive to keep some control over what happens to their creations.

Even closer to the New Zealand experience of small press publishing is Australia and Canada, although in terms of Government support for indigenous writing and publishing New Zealand is often somewhat behind its two Commonwealth sister countries. As elsewhere discussed in this thesis, the Canadians appear to have had an upturn in literary publishing in the early 1970's. For example grants from the Ontario Arts Council increased more than ten-fold from 0.43% of the total fund in 1969 to 5.44% in 1972. (see Table 3 for figures relating to numbers of books produced in NZ in these years) Also around this time people like poet and novelist Leonard Cohen, who several years earlier had been voted Canada's Young Poet of the Year, began to release albums with his writings set to music, thus further validating the sixties influence by marrying literature and contemporary music.

In 1973 a Royal Commission on Book Publishing in Canada exhorted the government to "seek to obtain as much prominence as possible for news and information regarding Canadian published books, through all appropriate media which it supports, including educational TV and official publications."[26] This pro-active approach to local literature can also be found in the small publishing scene in Australia.

Writing about the significance of the Literature Board of the Australia Council Michael Denholm states that "The importance of the Literature Board in the emergence of small publishers is demonstrated by the fact that prior to 1974, before it began funding authors in large numbers, there were hardly any viable small publishers in Australia."[27]

New Zealand small presses were at the same time trying to convince the government agencies that they were an important feature in NZ publishing. A report to the Department of Internal Affairs quotes from a submission "that the whole future of serious, creative literature lay in the activities of these small presses . . . The figures as cited by the New Zealand Book Publishers' Association for the year ending 31 March, 1975, state this fact very clearly. 'Token' publication of poetry, [by larger publishers] for example, is a lamentable fact. It's not the case with the small press publishers."[28]

---

1. Rosalie Carey, *A Theatre in the House: The Careys' Globe* (Dunedin: University of Otago Press, 1999), p 40.
2. Noel Waite, 'Private Printing', *Book & Print in New Zealand: A Guide to Print Culture in Aotearoa* (Wellington: Victoria University Press, 1997), p 82.
3. Questionnaire response - Hard Echo Press, Q6, p104.
4. Questionnaire response - Spiral Collective, Q1, p165.
5. Questionnaire response - Hawk Press, Q1, p108.
6. Questionnaire response - Hawk Press, Q6, p109.
7. Noel Waite, 'Private Printing', *Book & Print in NZ,* p 84.
8. Noel Waite, 'Private Printing', *Book & Print in NZ,* p 82
9. Mark Williams, 'Landfall: New Zealand's Longest-Running Literary Magazine,' *The Poet's Voice* (Salzburg) Vol. 2, No. 1, (June 1995), p 60.
10. Questionnaire response - One-Eyed Press, Q1, p132.
11. Questionnaire response - Prometheus Press, Q6, p154.

12. Questionnaire response - Pemmican Press, Q6, p150.
13. ***Oxford History of NZ Lit.***, 2nd ed. p 683.
14. Questionnaire response - Caveman Press, Q6, p89.
15. ***Book & Print in NZ***, p 156.
16. Questionnaire response - Hard Echo Press, Q6, p104.
17. Mark Pirie, ***New Zealand Writing: The NeXt Wave*** (Dunedin: University of Otago Press, 1998), Introduction, p 9.
18. Questionnaire response - HeadworX, Q7, p114.
19. Questionnaire response - Bumper Books, Q6, p80.
20. Questionnaire response - Original Books, Q6, p145.
21. Peter H. Mann, ***Book Publishing, Book Selling and Book Reading: A Report to the Book Marketing Council of the Publishers Association*** (London: Book Marketing Council, 1979), p 10.
22. Ian Norrie, ***Mumby's Publishing and Bookselling in the Twentieth Century*** 6th ed. (London: Bell and Hyman, 1982), p 106.
23. Questionnaire response - Bumper Books, Q8, p81.
24. Frederick G. Kilgour, ***The Evolution of the Book*** (New York: Oxford University Press, 1998), p 149.
25. Frederick G. Kilgour, ***The Evolution of the Book***, p 149.
26. Richard Rohmer, ***Canadian Publishers & Canadian Publishing*** (Ontario: Ministry of the Attorney General, 1973), p 263.
27. Michael Denholm, ***Small Press Publishing in Australia: the early 1970's*** (Sydney: Second Back Row Press, 1979), p 2.
28. O. St J. Vennell. ***Patronage and New Zealand Literature*** (Wellington: Department of Internal Affairs, 1976), p 15.

Epilogue

The fact that the majority of this thesis is given over to the small press bibliographies and the answers to the questionnaires sent out to the people involved is a statement about the kind of material presented. A careful reading of these documents will tell a lot about the situation encountered, the influences which affected each publisher and the circumstances under which each of them worked to bring much of our literature into printed reality. A good example of how a questionnaire can complement data is seen with John Denny's Puriri Press. His bibliography tells us that most of his titles, with his other imprint Pettifogging Press, are in editions of under 500.

However, what this fact does not tell us is the bearing this had on why Denny never applied for or received grants from the Literary Fund or Creative NZ. In his question response he states "I did consider asking for support once or twice, but was put off by the requirements for a minimum of 500 copies, a number which few of my publications reached."[1] With this small example we can see clearly the value of the questionnaire method in this case. If we look at the other bibliographies attached to the questions it becomes obvious that the vast majority of the titles published by the small presses involved were under 500 copies, thus precluding them from being able to apply for grants at least theoretically. So the issues which arise out of one sentence from John Denny are much more profound than if an hypothetical situation based on reading were proffered, at least in a thesis where the protagonists are still alive and where the majority of them are still active in small press publishing.

The aim of this thesis was very much in the nature of beginning a discussion. In fact I hoped to bring to the attention of people working in the field of New Zealand literature the extent and variety of small press publishing in this country. I also wanted to see how far there was truth in Michael Gifkins' assertion about the history of NZ literature being largely the history of small press publication which was quoted at the beginning of Chapter one of this thesis.

Many of the issues which have arisen out of my research can be seen as a starting point for further investigation. One example of this is the hypothesis in the first chapter regarding Māori publishing and possible reasons surrounding their difficulties with the printed word (for further consideration of why Māori didn't publish things until recently see Jane McRae in **Oxford History of New Zealand Literature,** 2nd ed.) The hints at early attempts to set up tribal and individual presses in the nineteenth century it is hoped will arouse the desire for further study. The effects of the music and ideas from the sixties can also be seen as a springboard to future investigation.

The effects of various governments' funding programmes for the arts is also a very significant issue which has barely been mentioned in the present survey but is obviously of considerable importance in relation to small press publishing. The fact that Trevor Reeves of Caveman Press is the only one of the twenty three respondents to the questionnaire who claim to have been appointed to the NZ Literary Fund Committee (in 1973) is of some concern. During his tenure he states "There was pressure to give grants to well-established presses rather than small private presses"[2] and this trend continues today where the overall percentage of funding is dropping steadily for small publishers (see Table 4).

Reeves continues "These days with the rapid rise of the 'corporate culture' the people making grants - mainly those trained in administration - are less likely to say 'what's the work like' and more, 'who the hell is he/she.'"[3] But, even with the difficulties of a small market-place, distribution, struggles of finance and lack of recognition the candid replies to the questionnaires show the majority of those involved in small press publishing will continue to produce the books they think need to be read.

This despite Denholm, quoting Australian Senator Susan Ryan, claiming in 1991 "that without specific government assistance, most of the 130 Australian publishing houses would be forced out of business transforming Australian cultural life into 'a small part of the enormous English language culture dominated by the USA and the UK.'"[4]

While similar fears were expressed throughout the eighties and nineties in New Zealand the reality saw a rise in certain types of new niche publishing ventures. Huia Publishers, for example, were specifically set up to publish Māori writers who may not have found a publisher otherwise. While they are set up more as a commercial business enterprise their market and choice of authors means that they may be seen in the context of a small publisher, although their end product is as good and professionally produced as any of the mainstream publishers. The same could be said for such firms as Steele Roberts who fall between the small press and professional publisher definition also.

Because this thesis deals with 'literary' publishers there are many other publishers such as George Griffiths of Otago Heritage Books who do not get mentioned although their *modis operandi* and other aspects of publishing are in many ways similar to their literary counterparts. Again publishers of local and regional histories, family histories and biographies using similar methods to the literary small presses all warrant study for their contribution to the 'Literature' of New Zealand Aotearoa.

The discrepancy between the acknowledged 'official' literature and the 'other' literature in New Zealand, is seen in the fact that, while there are nearly 300 authors published by the small number of presses represented in this survey (over a thirty year period), the total number covering the whole period of the time from 1830 represented in the ***Oxford Companion to New Zealand Literature*** published in 1998, is only 680 entries.

While it would be totally unrealistic to expect that such a broad based book as the ***Companion*** could include everyone who has written in this country the fact is that more than half the writers and poets in this survey are not mentioned in 'dispatches.' (see Table 5)

It is hoped by the presentation of this thesis that others will note the methods I have used and be encouraged to undertake further studies, either into individual presses or look at a more general thesis such as this one, to document the achievements of those who have made our literature come to life by their skill and commitment. One of the chief aims of this work is to show that in the literary history of New Zealand small presses have played a major role in presenting writers and poets to the reading public who larger, more commercial publishers may have ignored.

This opinion is corroborated by a leading study into alternative publishing in the wider world with reference to five of the leading literary figures of the twentieth century Eliot, Woolf, Joyce, Nin and Nabokov all of whom began their careers through small press or self publication. Having presented her case the author states, "These five cases are not unique. A look at the history of English-language literature reveals that alternative publishing, far from being unusual, is the usual path to prominence for writers whose work does not fit the contemporary commercial mold."[5]

It is clear from looking at the bibliographies and the answers to the questionnaires of the small press publishers presented in this thesis that the significance of small presses in the New Zealand literary scene over the past thirty years has indeed been the 'path to prominence' for many of the people involved. The period of the 1960's and the freeing up of ideas which, combined with the range of technologies available to the protagonists, lead to the upsurge in small press publishing which continues today.

In the poem on the death of John Lennon already quoted, ***Flip Side of the Ballad of John and Yoko***, there is a stanza which sums up aptly the effect of the sixties on the small press publishers in this study, whether high-brow or low-brow or in-between,

"Your songs and books helped me discover

In myself, what all the education in the world

Could not, that I could write and illustrate my own story"[6]

Add to that the word 'publish' and you have the story of Heather McPherson, Peter Olds, Bill Manhire, David Eggleton, Alan Brunton, Alan Loney Trevor Reeves and most of the other people surveyed in this thesis. The fact that they also published many of their own contemporaries shows the dedication to the literature of New Zealand Aotearoa these small publishers have displayed over many years.

---

1. Questionnaire response - Puriri Press, Q6, p160.
2. Questionnaire response - Caveman Press, Q4, p85.
3. Questionnaire response - Caveman Press, Q4, p85.
4. Michael Denholm, **Small Press Publishing in Australia: The late 1970's to the mid to late 1980's, Volume 2** (Footscray, Victoria: Footprint, 1991), p 23.
5. Sally Dennison, **(Alternative) Literary Publishing: Five Modern Histories.** (Iowa City: University of Iowa Press, 1984), p 193.
6. Michael O'Leary, **Flip Side of the Ballad of John and Yoko.** (Auckland: E.S.A.W., 1980), p 3.

Bibliographies and Questionnaire Replies

INCLUDES A BRIEF DESCRIPTION OF THE PRINCIPAL PEOPLE INVOLVED IN EACH SMALL PRESS AND, WHERE POSSIBLE, THE YEAR OF PUBLICATION AND THE NUMBER OF COPIES PRINTED FOR EACH PUBLICATION.

Publisher: Amphedesma Press

Bill Manhire (with Kevin Cunningham) Manhire is well known throughout N.Z. literary circles as a poet and academic critic, and his Creative Writing course at Victoria University. Possibly less known as a publisher, it can be seen by this list that, while small, his contribution in this field is significant.

BRUNTON, Alan, ***Messengers in Blackface,*** 1973, Poetry (200 copies)

IRELAND, Kevin, ***A Letter from Amsterdam***, 1972, Poetry (200 copies)

LIST, Dennis, ***A Kitset of 26 Poems***, 1972, Poetry (200 copies)

MANHIRE, Bill, ***Malady***, 1970, Poetry, with artwork by Ralph Hotere (200 copies)

ORR, Bob ***Blue Footpaths***, 1971, Poetry (200 copies)

SPIVEY, Anne, ***Relations***, 1973, Poetry (200 copies)

WEDDE, Ian, ***Homage to Matisse***, 1971, Poetry (200 copies)

WEDDE, Ian, ***Earthly: Sonnets for Carlos***, 1975, Poetry (450 copies)

1 - What was your initial reason for getting involved in publishing? Please try to think of this in the spirit of what you were thinking and doing at the time.

I think we all wanted to be publishers back in the late 60's. (And perhaps it was a bigger thing to aspire to in the days before office photocopiers and - now - cyberspace?). I had been involved in editing work: the ***Otago University Capping Book*** (with Russell Poole), the ***NZ Universities' Arts Festival Yearbook*** (with John Dickson). It seemed fairly normal to go on in some way or other.

In practice what happened was that I found myself in London in 1970, with the old desire now spurred on by nostalgia. A good friend of mine, and a fine poet, Kevin Cunningham, was also there. Kevin had access to an electric typewriter (two actually: one was a golfball job) - so we were high-tech, state-of-the-art. Kevin, now stricken with multiple sclerosis, is the secret genius in all this.

Our press got named in a somewhat accidental way. My ***Malady*** poem had been published - just after I left New Zealand - to coincide with Ralph Hotere's exhibition at Dunedin's Dawson's Gallery of a series of paintings based on the original poem. Someone - Ted Middleton, I think - thought of a publisher's name for the book. His idea was 'Amphidesma Press', which is somehow related to the toheroa. Somewhere along the line a spelling mistake got introduced, and Amphedesma Press was born. We simply stole the misprinted name.

2 - Who or what was your main influence behind your decision to publish? These may include literary or non-literary influences.

Paragraph one of the previous answer covers some of this. The other thing is that there genuinely were a whole lot of new writers around in the late 60's and early 70's. It was generational, of course, as Arthur Baysting's ***The Young New Zealand Poets*** asserted. But we felt there were people who hadn't been in print who ought to be.

So our first publications were – at least for people like Ian Wedde and Alan Brunton and Bob Orr – the writer's first publications. The first two of those writers were also in London in the early 70's, and friends – so I guess there's a degree of circumstance and accident about it all.

3 - In your choice of authors was the main consideration for inclusion philosophical, literary or pragmatic?

Pragmatic, I suspect. We published (mostly) stuff we liked and had somehow bumped into.

4 - "...and if there is still a number of commissioned works which seem to have been dreamed up by a sabotaging office-boy on an LSD trip, there are now each year a growing quantity of books which worthily add to our literature." Professor J.C. Reid from an article introducing New Zealand Books in Print, written in 1968. I interpret Reid's assessment as an indication of the rift between the acceptable 'worthy' literature as endorsed by academia, and the new wave of sabotaging office boys and girls who at that time commissioned publishers to put out their works, or simply published things themselves, and in many cases the work of their friends. Comment on this quote in relation to the 'Vanity Press' vs 'Real Publishing' debate.

Well, we sidestepped the 'vanity / real' debate by publishing none of our own work. On the broader question, a lot of the 'sabotaging office boys and girls' seem to end up being published by academic presses or taught in and endorsed by the academy. Even Alan Loney is published by Auckland University Press!

5 - Initially, was your focus outwardly cosmopolitan or inwardly New Zealand looking, and how has this emphasis changed over the years?

Well, we were in a big cosmopolitan place, but being very nationalistic in our behaviour. We didn't want to publish any 'English' poetry.

6 - What were your methods of printing and distribution as a publisher? Did you receive any financial or other assistance from either public organisations, or private sponsorship?

We had a sweet life; we never had to face the realities of the marketplace, whatever and wherever that was. Kevin Cunningham worked for the United Kingdom Council for Overseas Student Affairs. We used their office facilities (mostly the electric typewriters) to prepare photo-ready texts, and took them off to a local fast copy shop (these were just getting in London in the early 70's). We bought our own cover card – mostly in Tottenham Court Road at a place called (I think) Paperchase. We occasionally commissioned or found interesting covers: Neil Perrett did a cover for Kevin Ireland's Letters from Amsterdam. We nicked a Ralph Hotere drawing for Bob Orr's ***Blue Footpaths***. One of Penguin's illustrators did a cover for Anne Spivey.

Distribution was easy in our case. We had an arrangement with John Griffin of Dunedin's University Bookshop. He was a great facilitator and encourager of New Zealand writing. He agreed to buy all our copies more or less at cost. So once we had made the initial investment – i.e. the first payment to the fast copy shop – we always had enough money to cover the cost of the next publication. How far the books got distributed on from Dunedin, I don't know.

7 - How much of your publishing was commissioned and paid for (either fully or partially) by the author? Was your operation helped by the voluntary work of friends and family?

We contributed many hours of our own time – though we never thought of that as a cost. We never asked authors for any money. Mind you, we never paid the authors anything, either! None of the satisfaction had anything to do with money.

8 - What has been the cost to you personally in terms of time, money and resources, of being involved in publishing in New Zealand? You may consider this in relation to more difficult areas such as relationships with friends, family etc. also.

No cost at all. But then I never aspired to make a living as a publisher. I ended up sustaining myself through teaching: and all my writing, editing, and publishing have been subsidised by that working income.

So, to turn the question around, all my activity as a publisher has been pure gain. It has made my life more interesting, my friendships and connections more various.

9 - Where do you place yourself and your achievements as a publisher (and as a writer if applicable) in the history of the modern-day New Zealand literary scene? Do you feel that your contribution has been adequately acknowledged.

I think I'm probably over-acknowledged as a writer and – even more – as a teacher (the Victoria creative writing workshop). Probably as a publisher I'm less well known. Probably the thing I'm least known for, but where you might say my influence has been fairly extensive, is my work over the last twenty years for Victoria University Press.

B.M. Wellington, 2000.

Publisher: Bard Press + Gulf Coast + X-press it Press and Mainland Press, (plus collaborative work with Lancaster Publishing).

David Eggleton, well known throughout New Zealand as the Mad Kiwi Ranter, began publishing his own work to read at poetry readings especially during the 1980's.

Mainland and Gulf Coast Press

EGGLETON, David, ***Three Poems,*** 1978, Poetry broadsheet (300 copies)

EGGLETON, David, ***Backstreet Sideshow***, 1980, Poetry broadsheet (300 copies)

Bard Press

EGGLETON, David, ***Three Verse Epistles***, 1979, Poetry broadsheet (300 copies)

EGGLETON, David, ***Spirit of '79***, 1979, Poetry broadsheet (300 copies)

With Lancaster Publishing

EGGLETON, David, ***Dolebait (3 poems)***, 1982 Poetry broadsheet (400 copies)

EGGLETON, David, ***At the Crisis Centre (3 stories)***, 1982, Prose broadsheet (400 copies)

X-press it Press

EGGLETON, David, *The Mad Kiwi Ranter*, 1983, Poetry comic and political (500 copies)

EGGLETON, David, *The Mad Kiwi Ranter 2*, 1985, Poetry comic and political (500 copies)

Statement on self-publishing by David Eggleton

I began self-publishing in order not to have to structure my poetry according to the formats of the mainstream literary magazines in the late seventies and early eighties. I had long been inspired by the back-cover raves on the early Bob Dylan albums, and wanted to say similar things about urban life in New Zealand.

I found that by turning poetry into an active process of involvement via poetry readings, I was able to both create and interest an audience drawn from a wide cross-section of people.

Before too long I was travelling up and down the land, perching on tree stump or beer crate and declaiming verse to warm, even rapturous, applause. Invitations to read to schools, to tell my story on radio, to appear on T.V., began to trickle in. I made sure I always had a swag of pamphlets - broadsheets if you will - within easy reach in my trusty satchel. My first broadsheets sold for 40 cents, then 50, and ultimately I raised the price to a dollar a copy. Broadsheets were printed in coloured inks on white or manila card. Some ran into reprints.

The early eighties coincided with a poetry boom in a number of countries, and eventually I travelled to read my work at events in Australia, the U.S., the U.K., and Europe. In the nineties, however, poetry became marketed and commodified like everything else, and consequently marginalised. I no longer self-publish, but I do read, if invited.

D.E. Dunedin, 2000

Publisher: Black Robin Press.

Bill Wieben, a professional printer and typographer who has shown a dedication to publishing and the printed word for many years through his own press and through working with the Wai-te-ata Press.

BLUNT, Frances, ***When Leonardo Painted Trees: the Poems and Life of Frances Blunt of Kaikoura***, 1984, Poetry, edited by the author's sister, Joan Poulton

BURNS, Euan, ***Star Poems & Statements***, 1989. Poetry, with illustrations by Susan E. Burns

GILBERT, Ruth, ***Collected Poems***, 1987, Poetry (500 copies)

HAYWARD, Margaret, ***Hazel and the Golden Leaf***, 1985, Fiction with illustrations by Teresa Andrew (2575 copies)

JOHN, Edward, ***If You Can't Beat 'Em...***, 1993, Poetry (30 copies)

McQUEEN, Harvey, ***Oasis Motel and Other Poems***, 1986, Poetry (1560 copies)

McQUEEN, Harvey, ***Room, Room, Room***, 1989, Poetry (49 copies)

NOLAN, Iris, ***Bells for Caroline***, 1985, Fiction (1568 copies)

RABBITT, Lindsay, ***Set Piece***, 1984, Poetry

RABBITT, Lindsay, *Wayofit*, 1987, Poetry, with drawings by Jane Pountney

---

1 - What was your initial reason for getting involved in publishing? Please try to think of this in the spirit of what you were thinking and doing at the time.

1970: The first poetry I published was a concrete poetry compilation for the local university (California). They had no money and I had the facilities to do the work as a contribution to education - it was one of the first publications to include Charles Bukowski.

1981: When Reed moved to Auckland there had been many projects left stranded. As a book designer I had all the production tools to publish. Black Robin grew out of Puddlejump Design.

Black Robin is a tilt at Black Sparrow whose books I have always admired. Black Sparrow is also the publisher of Charles Bukowski. The name Black Robin was also a name Alan Loney and I had discussed using as a joint publishing name. Alan was in between publishing ventures. The later Black Light was his later venture after the joint venture did not proceed.

My wife and I decided that one [Black Robin] would be extinct at some time in the future - the bird or the company. Happily we are both here, but if I were a betting person I would give odds on the bird.

2 - Who or what was your main influence behind your decision to publish? These may include literary or non-literary influences.

The lack of established publishers interest in New Zealand literature in 1981. Corporate takeovers, bean counters and lack of commitment to literature.

3 - In your choice of authors was the main consideration for inclusion philosophical, literary or pragmatic?

Nearly all the publications in our list are there because I enjoyed the writing and wanted to see it published. If I were pragmatic I would have put the money on a horse!

4 - "...and if there is still a number of commissioned works which seem to have been dreamed up by a sabotaging office-boy on an LSD trip, there are now each year a growing quantity of books which worthily add to our literature." Professor J.C. Reid from an article introducing *New Zealand Books in Print*, written in 1968. I interpret Reid's assessment as an indication of the rift between the acceptable 'worthy' literature as endorsed by academia, and the new wave of sabotaging office boys and girls who at that time commissioned publishers to put out their works, or simply published things themselves, and in many cases the work of their friends. Comment on this quote in relation to the 'Vanity Press' vs 'Real Publishing' debate.

I don't give a damn about "endorsed by academia", and academia doesn't give a damn about me. We are square.

'Vanity Press' vs 'real publishing': Many colleagues of mine have noted that a smart money man (person) would or should never invest in publishing. The capital investment is too high for the returns. So most true publishers are doing so because they love the business.

There are not many books that are not Vanity Press to some degree. Authors - writing for very small if any returns.

Production - usually 1/4 to 1/2 the expenditure of a local annual report.

Publishers - small returns on investment hoping for a "big one" or two that will allow wages and expenses to be paid.

A good number of books are paid for by other books on a publishers list - Vanity Press?

5 - Initially, was your focus outwardly cosmopolitan or inwardly New Zealand looking, and how has this emphasis changed over the years?

Totally New Zealand and it hasn't changed. That way I avoid hostile takeovers.

6 - What were your methods of printing and distribution as a publisher? Did you receive any financial or other assistance from either public organisations, or private sponsorship?

I fund all publications and I sometimes do all the work myself. The exception to this is a book produced "on" or "by" commission.

7 - How much of your publishing was commissioned and paid for (either fully or partially) by the author? Was your operation helped by the voluntary work of friends and family?

A couple of the publications were commissioned for me to publish because they wanted me to publish their work.

Lots of voluntary work by my wife and friends.

8 - What has been the cost to you personally in terms of time, money and resources, of being involved in publishing in New Zealand? You may consider this in relation to more difficult areas such as relationships with friends, family etc. also.

The publishing Black Robin has done is always in partnership with all those concerned with each book.

Time, money, resources? It doesn't enter the publishing of a book. It is done or not done, and once done is complete without regret.

9 - Where do you place yourself and your achievements as a publisher (and as a writer if applicable) in the history of the modern-day New Zealand literary scene? Do you feel that your contribution has been adequately acknowledged.

Black Robin has done things a little differently from other publishers. The books are acknowledgement enough.

B.W. Wellington, 2000.

Publisher: Brick Row Publishers.

Ruth and Oz Kraus made a lasting impression on the New Zealand small publishing scene in the 1980's and 90's, not only for their own important publications but also by taking on the most difficult problem NZ publishers face, distribution. Thus Brick Row is cited throughout the period as being the distributor for many of the independent presses of the time and it is widely acknowledged that without them many of the literary works of the last twenty years would not have been as widely available as they were.

BREAM, Freda, *Island of Fear*, 1994, Novel (1000 copies)

BURTON & SMITH, *Oranges Skins are Free*, 1981, Poetry and photography p/b (100 copies) H/b (25 copies)

CLAPSHAW, Guy, *A Likely Story*, 1997, Autobiography (5000 copies)

EASON, Amanda, *Reasons for Loving*, 1994, Poetry (600 copies)

GADD, Bernard, ed., ***Other Voices***, 1989, Anthology (600 copies)

GADD, Bernard, ed., ***Other Voices 2***, 1991, Anthology (500 copies)

HORROCKS, Roger, ***Auckland Regional Poetry Transit Line***, 1982, Poetry (500 copies)

JOSEPH, M.K., ***Kaspar's Journey***, 1988, Novel, p/b (2000 copies) H/b (500 copies)

KRAUS, R.E. & O.L., eds., ***Other Voices 3***, 1993, Anthology (650 copies)

LOCKE, Elsie, ***Explorer Zach***, 1990, Fiction, with drawings by David Waddington (1500 copies)

MORRISSEY, Michael, ***Octavio's Last Invention***, 1991, Fiction (1000 copies)

ST. CARTMAIL, Keith, ***The World in Alphabetical Order***, 1993, Poetry (1000 copies)

SMITH, Miriam ***Ko Roimata me te Wao Nui a Tane***, 1986, Maori legends illustrated by Suzanne Walker (2000 copies)

SMITH, Miriam, ***Roimata and the Forest of Tane***, 1986, Māori legends illustrated by Suzanne Walker (2000 copies)

TRUSSELL, Denys, ***Walking into the Millennium and Shorter Poems***, 1998, Poetry (1500 copies)

JOURNALS

Parallax: 3 issues, 1982-83

PATERSON, Alistair ed., ***Poetry NZ***, 2000, Poetry (650 copies)

---

1 - What was your initial reason for getting involved in publishing? Please try to think of this in the spirit of what you were thinking and doing at the time.

I think I was born with a desire to be a publisher. At age 9, I was one of the many boys working in our spare time for the Curtis Publishing Co. selling subscriptions to the ***Saturday Evening Post***. My first real job in publishing was with the McGraw-Hill Book Co. in 1957 working in the 29 story green building on West 42nd. St., the first building in the U.S. built and designed for a publishing company. I joined the American Branch of Cambridge University Press in 1959 and remained with the world's oldest publishing house until I left for New Zealand in December, 1970. Ruth also did some interesting work at home for Cambridge. From the end of 1970 I was with A.H. and A.W. Reed, then New Zealand's premier publishing house, until I was fired 3 or 4 years later. Before establishing Brick Row I was engaged as a consultant by Stuart Parker then MD of Macmillan NZ and set up the first Macmillan distribution center in New Zealand. Brick Row began in 1977 and became a registered company, I think in 1977 or '78.

2 - Who or what was your main influence behind your decision to publish? These may include literary or non-literary influences.

I am enclosing a letter* which may answer this question and another one raised in your letter.

* The letter follows thus . . .

Books and publishers have been a life-long interest for me. I began collecting books when I learned to read before I was six. My father died when I was eleven and my mother was diagnosed with Parkinson's Disease in the same year. I guess reading was a kind of escape for me. I used to read all the books by my favourite author and then look up the publisher's address, take the subway downtown and call into the publisher's office to request a seasonal catalogue to see if any new books by my favourite author were scheduled for publication.

I discovered English literature in my early teens and began developing an interest in old editions. I often frequented second-hand bookshops until I discovered there were antiquarian booksellers who specialized in older books. I was given the name of a shop located on the fifth floor of a building on lower Fifth Avenue called The Brick Row Book Shop. I could not have been more than 15 or 16 years old at the time. The Shop was owned and operated by an elderly Irish scholar who seemed surprised by my interest in books and was very friendly. Most of the books which interested me were priced way beyond my means but I was delighted to examine and handle them. The owner, Byrne Hackett, became a friend and I remember visiting him on several occasions just to handle a first folio Shakespeare with price tag of $12,000. I found myself going down to visit The Brick Row Book Shop almost monthly and on several occasions Byrne Hackett took me to lunch at his favourite Italian restaurant. I think Byrne took a fatherly interest in me and gave me a real appreciation for old books. I believe he proved to be something of a romantic because a few years later he wanted me to meet a young lady who worked at the United Nations in New York. She had been educated in Ireland and was the younger daughter of an English earl. We met and dated a few times but I guess the chemistry wasn't there though Byrne said to me once that if I developed a serious interest in this girl and decided to marry he would let me have his summer country home as a honeymoon cottage.

Some years passed when I met Ruth and we married. The company I was working for closed down shortly after we married and when Byrne heard about it he sent us a very warm, sympathetic letter expressing his concern. After finding another job in a few weeks I thought it time to take Ruth downtown to meet Byrne

Hackett only to find that he had died. The shop was still open and the former assistant was packing things up.

Byrne Hackett had been with Yale University Press in 1915 when he was advised of the need for a scholarly second-hand bookshop for the Yale faculty. He opened such a shop in a building at Yale called Brick Row and later opened another at Harvard and a third at Princeton and then one in New York. All were closed after the depression except the one Fifth Avenue in New York. I named our publishing company in memory of Byrne Hackett as I knew he did not want the Brick Row Book Shop to continue after his death.

In San Francisco there was an antiquarian bookshop next to our hotel. They didn't have anything of interest to me but recommended another shop a few blocks away. Back in our room at the hotel I looked up the phone number in the yellow pages and discovered there was also a shop in the building called The Brick Row Book Shop!

I phoned and Ruth and I went over to meet the proprietor the next morning to find that it was indeed the original Brick Row Book Shop. Byrne Hackett's assistant bought the shop from his widow. He sold it a few years later to a man who moved it to Austin, Texas and then to San Francisco. It was then sold to the present owner who had a photograph of Byrne Hackett on the wall behind his desk. So our visit to San Francisco was not only a pleasant one but brought back lots of memories . . .

Letter ends.

3 - In your choice of authors was the main consideration for inclusion philosophical, literary or pragmatic?

Our choice in publishing was always literary which of course included philosophical. However most of our training in publishing came from Cambridge University and I guess I was influenced by the charter given to the university by Henry VIII in 1534 which was in fact a license to print and publish "all manner of books".

4 - "...and if there is still a number of commissioned works which seem to have been dreamed up by a sabotaging office-boy on an LSD trip, there are now each year a growing quantity of books which worthily add to our literature." Professor J.C. Reid from an article introducing *New Zealand Books in Print*, written in 1968. I interpret Reid's assessment as an indication of the rift between the acceptable 'worthy' literature as endorsed by academia, and the new wave of sabotaging office boys and girls who at that time commissioned publishers to put out their works, or simply published things themselves, and in many cases the work of their friends. Comment on this quote in relation to the 'Vanity Press' vs 'Real Publishing' debate.

I never presume to know exactly what is on a writer's mind, especially Professor Reid's. Nevertheless I have much to say about Vanity Press publishing. For many years I had nothing but contempt and scorn for vanity publishing. In the early years of Brick Row we were approached by several New Zealand writers who had books produced by a vanity press but we politely declined to distribute them. However as the shape of publishing changed in the later '70s most major NZ publishers were absorbed by the larger commercial publishing interests in Britain and Asia. New Zealand readers no longer had to wait a year after publication for popular books. Overseas publishers had a ready market in New Zealand enabling them to increase their print runs, reducing the unit costs of all their books. A small and relatively insignificant number of NZ authors were (and are) published by these houses but with very few exceptions the books of NZ authors got no further than New Zealand's shores. The overseas traffic was strictly one way! Even in the case of some of these authors, their work may not have been published without an Arts Council grant. Since market-led forces demanded a high rate of financial success it became nearly impossible for new writers to find a publisher. This became increasingly apparent to us at Brick Row but we employed a very old-fashioned publishing strategy.

Profits from successful books were used to subsidize worthwhile books we felt would probably not pay their own way.

We never engaged in vanity publishing but from then on we encouraged good writers to consider self publishing. Those who could afford to take our advice were guided by Brick Row through the intricacies of book design and other aspects of production. We never charged for this service but it was understood that Brick Row would have exclusive distribution rights. At one point we devised the Southern Lights imprint to distinguish these titles.

5 - Initially, was your focus outwardly cosmopolitan or inwardly New Zealand looking, and how has this emphasis changed over the years?

Our focus was always on New Zealand writers and New Zealand readers. However most of our revenue was derived from the distribution of the output of small NZ presses and from a few major American and British publishers. We were never successful in getting our own overseas publishers to take any New Zealand books. We were successful in bringing into New Zealand valuable books which otherwise would not have been found in New Zealand. These included self help books for children with learning difficulties, books for gifted children, books on teen suicide and professional books. NZ publishers who specialized in related areas were uninterested in these books owing to the small size of the market, while we found a ready market and did quite well with them. In the case of our poetry journal, **Poetry NZ**, we introduced some U.S., British, Australian writers and as a result found a small but growing market overseas and especially in the U.S. where I am promoting this journal at present.

6 - What were your methods of printing and distribution as a publisher? Did you receive any financial or other assistance from either public organisations, or private sponsorship?

We began to develop a distribution network before we published our first book. From about 1984 we used commission reps. We received Arts Council grants for a number of our books and journals, some assistance for one book from a public organization.

7 - How much of your publishing was commissioned and paid for (either fully or partially) by the author? Was your operation helped by the voluntary work of friends and family?

No publishing was ever commissioned or paid for by an author and we were never helped by voluntary work from anyone.

8 - What has been the cost to you personally in terms of time, money and resources, of being involved in publishing in New Zealand? You may consider this in relation to more difficult areas such as relationships with friends, family etc. also.

Brick Row began without any investment of capital and we introduced minimal funds only once or twice in the early days of Brick Row as bridging finance. Involvement in Brick Row, the extraordinary service we provided for customers, authors and would-be authors required almost all our time but the rewards in personal satisfaction in giving assistance in a small way to New Zealand literature, helping authors and proving to ourselves that we could do a better and more efficient job than our publishing colleagues, by far outweighed the cost of our time. I must confess, however, that although we had no plan to retire, by the time we reached our mid-70s I was beginning to tire a bit.

9 - Where do you place yourself and your achievements as a publisher (and as a writer if applicable) in the history of the modern-day New Zealand literary scene? Do you feel that your contribution has been adequately acknowledged.

Our contribution was never acknowledged except by one or two close friends who were aware of how much we were doing. However, we neither sought nor thought we deserved recognition. We kept too busy for such vanity.

O.K. Los Angeles, 2000.

Publisher: Bumper Books.

Alan Brunton, one of the acclaimed 'Red Mole' theatre group, has been publishing poetry and radical writings for many years. As the list below attests he is still active in bringing song lyrics and drama scripts into the realm of the printed page.

BRUNTON, Alan, ***Years Ago Today - Language and Performance: 1969***, 1998, NZ Cultural Studies:1

BRUNTON, Alan, ***'goin' to Djibouti'***, 1999, Legendary 1979 Red Mole playscript

BRUNTON, Alan, ***Moonshine***, 1999, Fiction

BRUNTON, Alan, ***Comrade Savage***, 2000, Playscript

BRUNTON, Alan, ***33 Perfumes of Pleasure***, 1998, Live performance CD with The Free Word Band

BRUNTON, Alan, ed., ***writing island bay***, 1996, Texts based on a show celebrating the Wellington seaside suburb

BRYANT, Rick, ***Clever Monkeys***, 1999, NZ Songwriter Series:1

EDMOND, Martin, ***Chemical Evolution: Art and drug culture***, 1998, NZ Cultural Studies: 2

HOFFMANN, Anna, *Tales of Anna Hoffmann, Part One*, 1998, Autobiography

HOFFMANN, Anna, *Tales of Anna Hoffmann, Part Two*, 1999, Autobiography

MELLING, G.J., *b. 1943*, 2000, Poetry and prose 1972 - 1999

RODWELL, Sally, *Heaven's Cloudy Smile*, 1999, Art video about the poetic imagination

RODWELL, Sally, *Zucchini Roma - A Life in the Theatre,* 1998, Autobiographical video with soundtrack by Jean McAllister

RODWELL, Sally, *Gonne, Strange, Charity*, 2000, Solo performance texts, edited by Alan Brunton

SAUNDERS, Barry, *White Man's Blues*, 1998, NZ Songwriters Series:2

SPITTLE, Gordon, *Beat Groups & Courtyard Parties*, 1994, New Zealand Music

YATES, Charlotte, *One Lady Driver*, 1998, NZ, Songwriters Series: 4

YOUNG, Mark, *The Right Foot of the Giant*, 1999, Poetry

JOURNALS

BRUNTON, Alan, ed., *Freed*, 1969, -72

BRUNTON, Alan, ed., *Spleen*, 1975, With Ian Wedde, -77

1 - What was your initial reason for getting involved in publishing? Please try to think of this in the spirit of what

you were thinking and doing at the time.

To control the means of production, to exorcise the demon of editorial censure, to prolong the infantile dream of liberty . . .

Inspired by stories of Baudelaire sleeping beneath the printer's press, as his magic incantations were reduced to ink and paper.

2 - Who or what was your main influence behind your decision to publish? These may include literary or non-literary influences.

The example of rock and roll artists controlling their own labels, e.g. the Beatles with Apple; Lewis and Pound with ***BLAST***; Ferlinghetti with City Lights Books; Jean Luc Godard and The Nouvelle Vogue movie scene coming out of France; 1968 graffiti during the "Days of Rage".

3 - In your choice of authors was the main consideration for inclusion philosophical, literary or pragmatic?

When Red Mole started to publish (books, magazines, records) it was to begin an across the board media empire! We published the first self-produced long-play record (***Across the Tracks***); e.p. (***Mr. Asia***); magazine (***Spleen***) and programmes for performance that contained theory and individual creative efforts, e.g. ***Oh Ravachol*** (1978).

4 - "...and if there is still a number of commissioned works which seem to have been dreamed up by a sabotaging office-boy on an LSD trip, there are now each year a growing quantity of books which worthily add to our literature." Professor J.C. Reid from an article introducing *New Zealand Books in Print*, written in 1968. I interpret Reid's assessment as an indication of the rift between the acceptable 'worthy' literature as endorsed by academia, and the new wave of sabotaging office boys

and girls who at that time commissioned publishers to
put out their works, or simply published things themselves, and in many cases the work of their friends.
Comment on this quote in relation to the 'Vanity Press' vs
'Real Publishing' debate.

All publishing in New Zealand is 'Vanity Press'; all publishers run to
Creative NZ; all publishing is personality-based and supported by
appeal to a schismatic market. Books that do not support New
Zealand's concept of nationalism are not published by 'real
publishers'.

**5 - Initially, was your focus outwardly cosmopolitan or
inwardly New Zealand looking, and how has this
emphasis changed over the years?**

Always cosmopolitan - desperately looking beyond the narrow
confines of a provincial and Anabaptist society; it remains so, but
with ironical references!

**6 - What were your methods of printing and distribution
as a publisher? Did you receive any financial or other
assistance from either public organisations, or private
sponsorship?**

All publications are self-financed - although the old Arts Council did
grant $40 to print ***Spleen*** once (1976). Distribution is by catalogue
& word of mouth; Bumper Books does not market. Our freedom
lies in the fact that the market comes to us. All the same, we are
open to individual donation - we appeal to guilt among the overly-
rewarded.

**7 - How much of your publishing was commissioned and
paid for (either fully or partially) by the author? Was your
operation helped by the voluntary work of friends and
family?**

All publishing is volunteer - it's the last area of amateurism in our society.

8 - What has been the cost to you personally in terms of time, money and resources, of being involved in publishing in New Zealand? You may consider this in relation to more difficult areas such as relationships with friends, family etc. also.

One does not count the cost - two might; that's why one must work alone.

9 - Where do you place yourself and your achievements as a publisher (and as a writer if applicable) in the history of the modern-day New Zealand literary scene? Do you feel that your contribution has been adequately acknowledged.

New Zealand does not have a literary scene; it has a 'writer's scene' which is different. All work is for the future . . .

A.B. Wellington, 2000.

Publisher: Caveman Press.

Trevor Reeves a poet and a printer who has worked tirelessly for many political as well as literary causes over more than thirty years. Presently he is involved in on-line publication on the internet, the highlight of which is an international literary review entitled *Southern Ocean Review* which Reeves edits. It also appears in a hard-copy edition.

BAXTER, James K., ***Ode to Auckland and Other Poems***, 1972, Poetry (2000 copies)

BAXTER, James K., **Letter to Peter Olds**, 1972, Poetry (100 copies)

BEYER, Tony, **Jesus Hobo**, 1971, Poetry (350 copies)

BEYER, Tony, **The Meat**, 1974, Poetry (150 copies)

BILLING, Graham, **The Primal Therapy of Tom Purslane**, 1980, Novel, (1000 copies)

BILLING, Graham, **Changing Countries**, 1980, Poetry (400 copies)

BROOKS, Jocelyn, **Ill Conceived**, 1981, Law and abortion practice in New Zealand (700 copies)

CARON, Elsa, et al., **Fri Alert**, 1974, Politics (3000 copies)

EDMOND, Murray, **Entering the Eye**, 1973, Poetry (400 copies)

ENSING, Riemke, ed., **Private Gardens**, 1977, An anthology of New Zealand women poets (1250 copies)

FOX, William L., **Trial Separation**, 1972, Poetry (400 copies)

GARDNER, Ray, **The Drug Book**, 1978, A drug addict's story (600 copies)

JOHNSON, Ingrid, **The Paper Midwife**, 1974, Home birth (2000 copies)

JOHNSON, Louis, **Onion**, 1972, Poetry (150 copies)

KEMP, Jan, **Against the Softness of Women**, 1973, Poetry (400 copies)

LASENBY, Jack, *Power*, 1972, Poetry (150 copies)

LIST, Dennis, *Pathways into the Brain*, 1973, Poetry (400 copies)

LONEY, Alan, *The Bare Remembrance*, 1971, Poetry (300 copies)

LONG, D.S., *Borrow Pit*, 1971, Poetry (350 copies)

MCALPINE, Rachel, *Stay at the Dinner Party*, 1977, Poetry (500 copies)

MCALPINE, Rachel, *Lament for Ariadne*, 1974, Poetry (500 copies)

MELLING, Gerald, *Open Schoolhouse*, 1980, Environments for children in N.Z., (1000 copies)

MELLING, Gerald, *Joyful Architecture*, 1980, The genius of New Zealand's Ian Athfield (1250 copies)

MITCALFE, Barry, *Migrant*, 1975, Poetry (400 copies)

MITCHELL, David, *Pipe Dreams in Ponsonby*, 1975, Poetry, 2nd ed. (400 copies), 1st ed. published by Stephen Chan, 1971

MORRISSEY, Michael, *Make Love in All the Rooms*, 1978, Poetry (400 copies)

NOAKES, John, *Life in N.Z.*, 1979, N.Z. Listener quotes & cartoons (2000 copies)

O'BRIEN, Karen, *Woman's Work*, 1981, Women at work (1000 copies)

OLDS, Peter, ***Lady Moss Revived***, 1972, Poetry (150 copies)

OLDS, Peter, ***4 V8 Poems***, 1972, Poetry (150 copies)

OLDS, Peter, ***Freeway***, 1974, Poetry (450 copies)

OLDS, Peter, ***Beethoven's Guitar***, 1980, Poetry (500 copies)

OLDS, Peter, ***Doctor's Rock***, 1976, Poetry (500 copies)

PATTERSON, Alistair, ***Cities and Strangers***, 1975, Poetry (500 copies)

REEVES, Trevor, ***Stones***, 1971, Poetry (600 copies)

REEVES, Trevor, ***Unemployment in the 1980's***, 1983, Politics (200 copies)

REEVES, Trevor, ***Apple Salt***, 1975, Poetry (500 copies)

ROWE, Rosamond Agnes, ***Feet Upon a Rock***, 1981, Autobiography (3000 copies)

SMITH, Hal, ***Divided We Stand***, 1981, Poetry (3000 copies)

SMITH, Lindsay, ***Skyhook***, 1971, Poetry (350 copies)

SOUTHAM, Barry, ***Mixed Singles***, 1981, Short stories (500 copies)

SOUTHAM, Barry, ***The People Dance***, 1982, Poetry (500 copies)

TUWHARE, Hone, ***Something Nothing***, 1974, Poetry (1000 copies)

TUWHARE, Hone, ***Come Rain, Hail***, 1973, Poetry (2000 copies)

TUWHARE, Hone, ***Sap-wood and Milk***, 1972, Poetry (3500 copies)

WANTLING, William, ***San Quentin's Stranger***, 1973, Poetry (800 copies)

WANTLING, William, ***Obscene and Other Poems***, 1972, Poetry (150 copies)

WRIGHT, Judith, ***The Fourth Quarter***, 1976, Poetry (400 copies)

1 - What was your initial reason for getting involved in publishing? Please try to think of this in the spirit of what you were thinking and doing at the time.

I had been writing poems and sending them off for publication for a while, and in the course of which, corresponded with Brian Turner who was at the time an editor with Oxford Press in Wellington. In a letter I received early in 1971 he told me he heard that I was about to set up a press. That was news to me, but I thought "why not," so I wrote down the name of my press that simply popped into my head at the time: Caveman Press.

2 - Who or what was your main influence behind your decision to publish? These may include literary or non-literary influences.

My main influence was Lindsay Smith who, through the 60's had been a music student at Otago University. He also wrote poetry and in the course of our friendship I became interested in doing that too - having given up any idea of continuing with my music interests. His book of poems ***Skyhook*** was ready for publication, and I decided to publish it. My brother, Graeme, an accountant, took an interest in the finances and to some extent distribution of Caveman Press. We acquired a 1914 Golding Platen disc-inker letterpress machine as a donation from Whitcoulls and I learned how to do letterpress printing, firstly using handset type, and later linotype. Alan Loney joined us in late 1971 and handset his own book, and was a helpful influence as we progressed.

3 - In your choice of authors was the main consideration for inclusion philosophical, literary or pragmatic?

I think literary was the principal consideration in choice of work to publish. However, we did take a policy direction which included publishing the work of overseas writers. A principal influence was my association with Don Long, an American who came to New Zealand with his parents at the age of 14. He wrote a lot of poetry, eventually setting up ***Edge*** magazine, which published a lot of overseas work. We were not interested in philosophical directions in the writing, specifically.

The main criteria being that it must be creative. Nor were we interested in 'movements' such as post-modernism etc. We were not university orientated but on the other hand, we did not exclude ourselves from their influences. Another influence in our choice of authors was to see if we could include graphic material to complement the written work.

We did this successfully with artwork complementing books by the likes of Stanley Palmer (Tony Beyer), Ralph Hotere (Hone Tuwhare) and Barry Cleavin (Lindsay Smith) etc. To an extent we were 'creating' our own market for poetry collections, so the pragmatism of choosing already successful authors did not really enter into our calculations.

4 - "...and if there is still a number of commissioned works which seem to have been dreamed up by a sabotaging office-boy on an LSD trip, there are now each year a growing quantity of books which worthily add to our literature." Professor J.C. Reid from an article introducing *New Zealand Books in Print*, written in 1968. I interpret Reid's assessment as an indication of the rift

between the acceptable 'worthy' literature as endorsed by academia, and the new wave of sabotaging office boys and girls who at that time commissioned publishers to put out their works, or simply published things themselves, and in many cases the work of their friends. Comment on this quote in relation to the 'Vanity Press' vs 'Real Publishing' debate.

To a large extent literature has never been the exclusive preserve of academia, although issues of 'professionalism' continually arose in the 60's and 70's and even later, where academics liked to suggest that writing of superior quality arose out of the academic process. There are elements of truth in this, but traditionally, the bulk of truly great writing comes from no really specific area of society. This is particularly true of American writing where nationalism is not an obsession such as it has been in New Zealand and Canada and some other countries. Also the grants systems in New Zealand and Canada tend to favour writing by academics, for academics.

In general, there is a sort of levelling-out phenomenon in place in any society, so that bad work, whether it be academically derived, or those by 'ordinary members of the public' (for want of a better description) will ultimately be seen for what it is - good or bad; popular or shunned.

Funding has always been a problem for literature. Funders, for instance the Literary Fund, which was replaced by the Q.E.2 Arts Council, then Creative New Zealand, had always been starved for funds. I was appointed to the N.Z. Literary Fund Committee in 1973 for a three year term, and in those days we had no more than $4,500 each year to dispense.

There was pressure to give grants to well-established presses rather than small private presses, which was probably fair enough, but I can say that the emphasis has now changed quite a lot. In those days there were people on the committee who knew writing well but came, not just from the universities, but from publishing, bookselling, schools etc.

These days with the rapid rise of the 'corporate culture' the people making grants - mainly those trained in administration - are less likely to say 'what's the work like' and more, 'who the hell is he/she.'

As to the "Vanity Press" there has always been a lot of that, and even more these days. In fact, because of the decline of printed literature (for instance 90% of all New Zealand's bookshops are owned by one man), and the rise of the Internet, printed books are more often than not subsidised by their authors, or paid for in full by them. However, that includes books by academics, particularly in the non-fiction field.

Also there is the advent of printing technology which enables you to go to a printer with a computer disk and ask the printer to 'docutech' 200 copies please - all at a reasonable cost. I am presently doing this for authors with the press that succeeded Caveman Press, Square One Press.

I believe "real publishing" is just that - any sort of publishing is real publishing, whether it is on-line on the Internet or even on C.D's. I don't think the term "Vanity Press" has much currency any more. You can spend six months writing a book, give the manuscript to a publisher who publishes it at his own expense, perhaps with the aid of a grant, then get no return at all in terms of royalty as a return for the work you put in. Is that "Vanity Publishing"? Or you could put up the printing cost, then go halves with the publisher on the sales of the book, after he has paid the distribution cost - and still make no return on your efforts. In a sense , all publishing is vanity and the methods by which the publishing is done do not change it from being just that. So you might as well call vanity publishing, real publishing.

Some publishers have a different view. For instance, the publishers who award the Pushcart Prize in the U.S.A. deliberately exclude from consideration any work that has appeared solely on the Internet, claiming that this work is "Vanity" publishing. Of course it isn't, because somebody has to pay for it, and more likely than not the author doesn't get a return just in the same way as he gets little or no return in the ways described above, from print publishing.

The New Zealand Society of Authors (PEN) are seeking to establish their membership status criteria in that writers who are published on Internet magazine (of which there are thousands throughout the world, now) as insufficient reason to allow them ordinary membership. I believe this is divisive and backward-looking. Literature endorsed by academia has, in my opinion, no more claim to quality than non-academic literature not endorsed by academia. An example is the work of American writer Charles Bukowski, who never went near a university in his life.

However, his books are the most borrowed works of literature in USA libraries, both public and academic. His works beat the rest, hands down. If you bring up the subject of Bukowski in library lists on the Internet, such as "Cafe Blue" a university-based university list, you will get a diatribe of abuse, as I have received. Bukowski came through the "wrong door" and is deeply resented.

In New Zealand you have the modest example of Alan Duff (did I say modest?) whose work is not academically based or accepted, breaking sales records. Things have moved along from the days of J.C. Reid, although I would have no criticism of his worth and place in New Zealand literature. A fine writer and editor, indeed.

However, some academics are still maintaining the "myth of difference" and various policies of exclusion. A case in point was the publication of the **Oxford Companion of New Zealand Literature** in 1999. A whole chunk of writers and publishers from the early to mid 1970's and even later, were omitted, including myself and Caveman Press. Also other presses at the time that had broken the 'nationalistic' mould and reached outside New Zealand to publish, were excluded. Surprise omissions include Jim Henderson and even a former holder of the Burns Literary Fellowship at Otago University, John Dickson! Spectacularly missing was Stephen Higginson (who at one time was an editor and writer at Caveman Press), and his magazine, **Pilgrims**. It was not easy to contemplate that this was the result of incompetence. One instance was a mention of **Private Gardens**, New Zealand's first anthology of poetry for women poets - published by Caveman Press in 1977. Not only did this highly regarded and completely sold out book get scant attention in the ***Oxford Companion***, but the editors did not even have the courtesy to attribute the publication to Caveman Press - so Caveman couldn't even make it into the index, even on those grounds! Oxford's web site has done a bit of a "catch-up" of some of the more glaring omissions, but not of any significance.

5 - Initially, was your focus outwardly cosmopolitan or inwardly New Zealand looking, and how has this emphasis changed over the years?

Initially, the focus of Caveman Press was inward focussing - local authors etc., but became outwardly cosmopolitan in response to what could be described as a literary movement - not academically based, I might add, to contrast the work of overseas with what writers here were producing. The aim of this was to try to broaden the range of subject matter and modify the influence of those who were looking for the "Great New Zealand Novel" to "The Great Novel". This was my focus right up until Caveman Press ceased publishing literature to concentrate on publishing general books of non-fiction, in the early 1980's.

With the demise of other magazines and publishers in the 1980's things quickly returned to "normal", where the inward looking past had re-established itself with the help of academia, which had been affronted by the "office boy" publishers. In fact I was an office boy in a wool store until I threw in the job in 1974 to become a full-time publisher.

At that time I was appointed to the N.Z. Literary Fund through the influence of Patricia Godsiff, then retired as a Nelson school headmistress. That appointment enraged some writers who considered themselves firmly established and calling the shots. Two of these, O.E. Middleton and [——], tried to browbeat and cajole me into relinquishing the appointment. They may have won in the end, after Middleton set up a petition to ask the Minister of Internal Affairs to have me removed. I was not re-appointed.

With the advent of the Internet in the early 1990's, literature became more global. More overseas writers began being published in New Zealand magazines - both on-line (although my **Southern Ocean Review** is still really the only international one), and in print (**Takahe, Jaam** etc.), but not in **Landfall** and **Sport**. However, the definite up-side was that more New Zealand writers were publishing in overseas magazines - particularly magazines on the Internet. This was especially gratifying, because even though most Internet magazines are based in the USA and are already internationally focused, New Zealand writers are making it into these publications against very stiff competition indeed. This can only help raise the standard of New Zealand writing published here in New Zealand, and indeed this is happening now.

The "outward-looking" revolution that began in the early 1970's has resumed. The younger generation of writers and publishers, such as Mark Pirie, seem prepared to continue it. Creative New Zealand, of course, is still reluctant to fund publications with overseas content in them - even though the New Zealand writers may be getting substantial overseas coverage in them.

Such considerations do not affect funding in, say, the USA, where the criteria is whether the content is worthy or not, not where it comes from.

6 - What were your methods of printing and distribution as a publisher? Did you receive any financial or other assistance from either public organisations, or private sponsorship?

With Caveman Press there were some grants applied for and received, but not many. We received no assistance from public organisations, and only a little from private donations. Sales of poetry in those days were buoyant, and there was no significant shortfalls in returns. **Private Gardens** for instance, although well funded, sold 1275 copies - a pleasing result. Also, in those days there were few photocopiers, so copyright was not significantly breached as is the case these days, particularly with the advent of the Internet.

Methods of printing in the early days of Caveman Press began with handsetting letterpress, then linotype, with all the production being done "in house". This changed later to using regular printers using offset with type and paste-ups supplied. Later, we used overseas printers where there was a need to do overseas imprints for publishers overseas (such as a Graham Billing novel we published). These days the wheel has turned full circle, with the shrinkage of demand for printed collections of poetry for instance. Small runs of books - say, 50 - 100 copies, can now be done on a high quality photocopy machine. An example is the 50 copies on paper we publish every issue of ***Southern Ocean Review***, concurrent with the Internet version, which so far has received over 20,000 "hits". In an age where the booksellers' monopoly will not stock poetry books on principle, private distribution by mail order, supply to libraries, and publishing on the Internet is the order of the day.

7 - How much of your publishing was commissioned and paid for (either fully or partially) by the author? Was your operation helped by the voluntary work of friends and family?

In the 1970's none of our work was commissioned or paid for. We are looking at this now, however, as the market for printed books continues to shrink. The publishing operation then certainly benefited from the voluntary help of friends and family. Later in the 1970's, with a publishing office and other activities developed such as graphic design and marketing - and also with book importation - our publishing became more professionally based, employing editors and people to help with distribution.

8 - What has been the cost to you personally in terms of time, money and resources, of being involved in publishing in New Zealand? You may consider this in relation to more difficult areas such as relationships with friends, family etc. also.

In terms of time and money, we had some successes and some failures. In terms of money, we always made money from publishing and distribution overall - at least until the exchange rate reverses in 1981 - 82 which left us (along with other distributors such Fullertons) no alternative but to cease publishing and distributing under that imprint. Square One Press was established later in that decade (80's) and we are still going today. I never begrudged any time I put into writing and publishing. Even less so now, as the urge or need to 'earn' a living is now more or less absent.

9 - Where do you place yourself and your achievements as a publisher (and as a writer if applicable) in the history of the modern-day New Zealand literary scene? Do you feel that your contribution has been adequately acknowledged.

Having no place set for my activities in publishing and writing by the ***Oxford Companion to New Zealand Literature***, it is difficult to assess my achievements as a writer and a publisher. As a writer I believe I made some considerable headway in the short fiction milieu, having had stories placed overseas in print and Internet magazines - some for quite considerable payments, even on the Internet. My publisher (HeadworX) had applied for a Creative N.Z. grant for my book of short stories, ***Breaker Breaker and Other Stories*** but there is no guarantee of success there, as they may decide that since my work is not well known here, it is no good. (In fact, it was subsequently turned down.) Corporate managers now read the manuscripts (if indeed that is what they do) and they may well decide that Te Papa or the Edinburgh Tattoo is worthy of more money than my little book.

At one stage Caveman Press in the mid-1970's was publishing half the total books of poetry published in New Zealand. With other publishers at the time, mostly young, we were up to the three quarter mark, I estimate.

I am heartened by the "young crop" of writers and publishers coming along. They are a realistic lot and I learn from them, now, in terms of the technologies of publication and distribution. Some have had to step over high hurdles set by established academics, when in fact they are academics too. It seems to be a different scene.

One of the tools of academia is to set up writing courses. This is practiced widely in America, and we have our breed of it in New Zealand. I am not against this, as surely the arts faculties need more encouragement in this age of corporate utilitarianism where the funding favours buildings and institutions rather than creative individualism. A lot of the work submitted from American poets with Ph.D's or MFA's in creative writing is pretty pedestrian, convoluted, or drearily negative.

A lot of the writing courses carefully teach bad writers on how to become mediocre ones. Well, mediocre ones can become better ones, so maybe we need those writing courses. But it would be a mistake to say that those who didn't attend writing courses are mediocre writers or worse, never to become really good writers.

We really need some unbiased and objective commentators on the general overall scene in literature in this country. From a general perspective and not via an academic viewpoint. I am hopeful.

T.R. Dunedin, 2000.

Publisher: Hallard Press.

Bernard Gadd is a South Auckland poet, novelist and publisher. Also includes Hillary Press and Te Ropu Kahurangi. Gadd has been significant in publishing and writing works which working-class, urban Māori, and Polynesian people can relate to.

BOSTOK, Janice, **Shadow-Patches**, 1998, Haibun, with Bernard Gadd and Catherine Mair (150 copies)

ESPINOZA, E., **An Elegy to Hope**, 1991, Poetry, in Spanish and English (250 copies)

GADD, Bernard, ***Childsong and other Verses***, 1981, Poetry (50 copies)

GADD, Bernard, ***Two Poems***, 1981, Poetry (50 copies)

GADD, Bernard, ***Light***, 1985, Poetry, prints by Ruth Davey (150 copies)

*GADD, Bernard, ***Blood of Tainui***, 1990, Novel (700 copies)

GADD, Bernard, ***Just Like You Said It Would Be***, 1992, Stories (250 copies)

GADD, Bernard, ***Pity Mr. Hash***, 1995, Satirical verse, art by Anna Tarm (120 copies)

GADD, Bernard, ***Thornend***, 1995, Stories, future fantasy (50 copies)

GADD, Bernard, ***Catullus at the Iron Gate***, 1995, Poetry, art by Eun Kyoung Kim Eo (70 copies)

GADD, Bernard, ***I Imagines Serifim***, 1999, Poetry (50 copies)

GADD, Bernard, ***Signs of the New Right***, 2000, Satirical poetry (50 copies)

*GADD, Bernard, ed., ***Other Voices***, 1989, Anthology of new writing in N.Z. (500 copies)

*GADD, Bernard, ed., ***Other Voices 2***, 1991, Anthology of prose and verse (300 copies)

GADD, Bernard, ed., ***Catching the Light***, 1992, Poetry, by eight writers (300 copies)

*JOSEPH, M.K., ***Kaspar's Journey***, 1988, Novel (1000 copies)

LEWIS, Flossie, ***Who wants to be Lillian Plotnick's Mother?***, 1981, Stories, with Bernard Gadd (300 copies)

*** With Brick Row**

LING-YEN, ***Conversations in the Bathtub***, 1989, Poetry (150 copies)

O'CONNOR, John, ***Too Right Mate***, 1996, Satirical verse, with Bernard Gadd, art by Anna Tarm (200 copies)

As Hillary Press

GADD, Bernard, ***Melissa***, 1980, Poetry (80 copies)

GADD, Bernard, ***Run Ue Run***, 1980, Novelette

WERATA, Tama, ***Dark Way Home***, 1982, Novel

As Te Ropu Kahurangi

GADD, Bernard, ***Tokerau and Other Stories***, 1984, Short stories (100 copies)

GADD, Bernard, ***Laya***, 1985, Novel, cover art Ruth Davey (300 copies)

GADD, Bernard, ***Dare Not Fail***, 1987, Novel, cover art Ruth Davey (750 copies)

JOHNS, Atihana, ***Just Wondering***, 1986, Short stories, drawings by Kura Rewiri-Thorsen

KAURAKA, Kauraka, *Na Fakahiti O Manihiki*, 1988, Traditional narratives, myths and legends retold in Manihikian and English. Artwork by Rennie Peyroux

JOURNALS

GADD, Bernard, ed., *SPIN*, 1998, Poetry, magazine with Catherine Mair (160 copies)

GADD, Bernard, ed., *SPIN*, 1999, Poetry, magazine with Catherine Mair (180 copies)

1 - What was your initial reason for getting involved in publishing? Please try to think of this in the spirit of what you were thinking and doing at the time.

(a) As head of the English Department arriving in 1971 at Hillary College in Otara I soon found a need to provide literature for working class - and especially working class Māori and Polynesian families - both school attendees, and school leavers and adults. The stocks of books I inherited as HOD at the school included stuff like *Lyrical Ballads* by Wordsworth and Coleridge, Bulldog Drummond etc. I began by looking for stories to collect into an anthology to use as a classroom text, and two collections resulted, *My New Zealand One* and *Two* published by Longman Paul about 1973. But there was little suitable material, and even if anything was by working class writers, it was written for the "Boss classes". I decided to do two things: write stories myself, and find writers especially those who could not get published often or at all by commercial publishers, to include in anthologies for school or general use, or to publish collections of their own works.

Hence the books by Atihana Johns and the late Kauraka Kauraka. The *Other Voices* collections included little known writers Reihana MacDonald, Momoe von Reiche, Saneha Lauckaphone, Mererana Curie, Gilbert Haisman, Peter Payne, and helped to give Hone Tuwhare, Cherie Barford, L.E. Scott, David Eggleton,

Leanne Radojkovich, and others some attention. Of course I was doing this through publications published by other people, e.g. ***Pacific Voices, New Zealand Now.***

(b) I wanted to help into print writers with strong things to say which it was not always easy to find publishers for. Hence the books by Estaban Espinoza, a Chilean refugee, and Ling-yen, a young Chinese, Flossie Lewis, an American well known in the San Francisco area but not at all known here, and M.K. Joseph, a writer studiously neglected by academia (he had harsh things to say about his fellow academics in his day) - he left three books unpublished at his death, two of them in ms form.

(c) I wanted to see some specifically left-wing, non-polemical literature in print . . . hence work by Peter Payne, John O'Connor, Hone Tuwhare, David Eggleton, Estaban Espinoza, Joanna Mary, not to mention M. O'Leary, and my own political satires.

(d) And I wanted to get my own work, fiction and poetry, into print, finding that most of it was unacceptable to commercial publishers.

(e) And like most publishers I enjoyed getting new writers into print for the first time, such as teenagers (at the time) Anne Martin and Tiara Lowndes, or literacy class graduate Mercana Curie.

2 - Who or what was your main influence behind your decision to publish? These may include literary or non-literary influences.

(a) The needs I perceived the Hillary College youngsters to have was a major influence. Te Ropu Kahurangi proved to be a good instrument for such publication, particularly helpful was the interaction among members who included an HOD English, an English teacher-artist, a Māori language teacher, and the school reading teacher. We made plans and carried them through, e.g. the idea of my writing a series of fiction works to cover Māori history from the Lapita days (c. 1500 BC) to the present.

(b) The 1970's were quite a hey day for the slim poetry or fiction volume from small presses. I was impressed by the work of Alistair Taylor, e.g. his productions of Alistair Campbell's works, Trevor Reeves at Caveman with his production of Tuwhare poems and others, **Outrigger** with its cheap format volumes, Norman Simms with his slim volumes often of overseas writers, and the self-published work of e.g. Alistair Campbell (I think the first was **The Dark Lord of Savaiki**). Al Wendt and Hone Tuwhare sometimes sent me copies of slim collections of poetry from the Pacific Islands, notably from Mana Press in Fiji and from New Guinea. I also encountered on a visit to the U.S. with an international group of educators in the 1970's, the slim but high quality productions of a Native American press in Seattle producing for the Warm Springs Reservation, as well as school resources produced by the Chinese bi-lingual school in San Francisco. Aboriginal groups were also producing small books in their languages. All this inspired me to do the same through both Hallard Press and Te Ropu Kahurangi.

(c) As far as publication of my own work was concerned, by the 1970's and 80's I was getting verse and stories into mags such as **Mate** and its successors, **Landfall** (under the editorship of Peter Sharp . . . but never since!), **Te Ao Hou**, **Northland** and decided that I was writing enough to publish my own little booklets. Of course, when looking back now I think some were not worth the effort, but others definitely were e.g.. **Melissa, Catullus**.

(d) And of course the commercial publishing industry in NZ exerted its own influence. NZ has always had claques of academics, pens-for-hire, editors, wielders of power in our little literary world who acted to advance their own interests including those of their "clients", lovers, students, mates etc. But during the 1970's even publishing houses bought out by larger firms - such as Longman Paul - were willing to take a punt on many kinds of writing and writers. The willingness steadily reduced as the New Right era advanced and local publishers were taken over by huge trans-national corporations, and accountants ruled the roost. Simultaneously many of the older magazines died, and those surviving and the new ones were often edited by conventional or conservative minds, or who were simply academic snobs.

3 - In your choice of authors was the main consideration for inclusion philosophical, literary or pragmatic?``

All of those elements were important. As Te Ropu Kahurangi publisher I was primarily interested in getting into print writers who could appeal to working class and Māori and Polynesian teens and adults, and who could write with what I considered authenticity about their lives and backgrounds. I developed a large net of contacts here and abroad, including people like Johns, Tuwhare, and others included in my various anthologies. As a result Atihaha Johns, Estaban Espinoza and Kauraka Kauraka approached me to see if I was interested to publish collections they had found commercial publishers were not interested in. Similarly Ling-yen approached me with her project.

As Hallard Press and when working with Brick Row I was interested in getting into print new writers, little known writers, left-wing writers and Māori, Polynesian, Asian writers.

A quite different and smaller network grew as I came into contact with other poets, notably those now associated with Sudden Valley Press in Christchurch and the magazine **SPIN**. Many of these shared an interest in haiku and other Japanese derived genre. These were the people who formed the core of the poets in **Catching the Light** and more recently **shadow-patches**.

I'm sure all other small press publishers also are invited by writers fresh from some creative writing class to pay for the glossy publication of their proffered works and to hand over payment for the privilege of doing so. I turn all down. These days on my much reduced income and into my impatient 60's, I am only interested in publishing myself and my mates and following my own star.

4 - "...and if there is still a number of commissioned works which seem to have been dreamed up by a sabotaging office-boy on an LSD trip, there are now each year a growing quantity of books which worthily add to our literature." Professor J.C. Reid from an article introducing *New Zealand Books in Print*, written in 1968. I interpret Reid's assessment as an indication of the rift between the acceptable 'worthy' literature as endorsed by academia, and the new wave of sabotaging office boys and girls who at that time commissioned publishers to put out their works, or simply published things themselves, and in many cases the work of their friends. Comment on this quote in relation to the 'Vanity Press' vs 'Real Publishing' debate.

I actually read John Reid's comments differently . . . I wonder if he was referring as "office boys" to people like book packagers and publishing brokers and pens-for-hire who dream up books for the sole purpose of turning a profit e.g.. collections of historical materials ripped out of old mags and newspapers, coffee table productions, anthologies of the ilk of ***Love Stories by Butch Thai Lesbians*** and ***The Collected Speeches of Sir Small Fart*** for small but affluent readerships, and so on.

I think the real division is not between Vanity Press and the others - after all, many writers self-publish even if they have to call themselves So and So University Press e.g.. Stead. Some like Hone Tuwhare are lucky enough to have friends willing to publish at no cost.

I think the division is an artifact of the existence of glitterati cliques who grab the purses and positions of power and influence in the literary world and those interested in it.

It is these literary power brokers who try to lay down (especially for the media and naive school teachers and lazy uni lecturers) who is regarded as belonging on the list of REAL WRITERS or regulated to the list of INFERIOR WRITERS. The REAL WRITERS are those who are successful commercially or in getting attention for themselves. Of course some of these REAL WRITERS actually are good writers, but people like Anne French, Bill Manhire usually are not but have been hyped up by their media friends.

I think the sad thing about NZ literature today is the tiny numbers of saboteurs of the self-opinion of the glitterati let alone of things traditional, conventional, conservative. So many of the rising Generation X are instinctive Tories.

I have no problem with being a Vanity Press writer. My problem is with the lousy job the commercial publishers are doing.

5 - Initially, was your focus outwardly cosmopolitan or inwardly New Zealand looking, and how has this emphasis changed over the years?

Both inward and cosmopolitan. As regards NZ writing I was from the start and still am interested in encouraging the literature of dissent whether it be from people of minority ethnicities, working class writing, or critical satirical or leftist writing.

Since I retired from secondary teaching in 1987 I have become more intensively involved in poetry publication and writing, hence *Catching the Light* and *shadow-patches*. **SPIN** magazine and especially ***winterSPIN*** has developed into an international magazine attracting world-class writers of haiku etc. and writers from many countries, as well as known names from NZ such as Riemke Ensing, John O'Connor, John Allison.

I don't really think the balance of my publishing has changed. In 1981 I published a book of stories of an American writer and myself, and today I have been typing onto my computer work for the forthcoming ***winterSPIN*** issue from a Giovanni Malito from Ireland (No kidding.)

6 - What were your methods of printing and distribution as a publisher? Did you receive any financial or other assistance from either public organisations, or private sponsorship?

I have always looked for an independent small printer who can do things cheaply. But these days rapid Xerox and such printing methods mean that many printers can offer to do short runs cheaply. Currently I am using Massey University printery.

For distribution of poetry I try to do it myself, sometimes placing flyers in **winterSPIN**. But until they closed down I always used Brick Row who distributed to bookshops and sometimes had standing orders from libraries. No one has replaced Brick Row, and I miss their services. I have built up a bit of a list of potential buyers over the years, but it is hard to sell poetry . . . there is so much available.

I have as noted on the book list received a few grants from the QE 2 arts council. And Kauraka Kauraka tickled mysterious Cook Island funds. And Espinoza in part and Ling-yen in full paid for their productions. Other than that, no funding nor sponsorships.

7 - How much of your publishing was commissioned and paid for (either fully or partially) by the author? Was your operation helped by the voluntary work of friends and family?

As shown on the book-list. The authors approached me and had funding available. One author (Johns) I published without asking for any funding from him. For **shadow-patches** we three authors shared the costs and incomes. For **Kaspar's Journey** Brick Row and I shared the costs and income. (It never paid for itself.)

But I have decided that on the whole it is too much hassle and too much of a gamble to publish other people's work, so stick to my own and that of people I know well.

Yes my wife always helped with proof-reading and collation in the days when those were necessary. And much of Te Ropu Kahu-rangi's work involved at least some joint effort by all members. But as the years went by I became the only one actively involved in Te Ropu so I closed the thing down and divided the profits among us.

8 - What has been the cost to you personally in terms of time, money and resources, of being involved in publishing in New Zealand? You may consider this in relation to more difficult areas such as relationships with friends, family etc. also.

The cost has changed according to my circumstances, the amount of publishing I was doing, and the available technology. While I was teaching (the 1980 - 87 period) it was sometimes very stressful. I had a busy job; there was much hand work to be done such as collating and even to staple and trim. Travel was involved when I was using the Auckland Teachers Resource Centre printery and later on Priority Press in Hamilton.

With Brick Row the work could be divided up. But my wife always assisted with proof-reading and sometimes collating in the earliest days, as well as mailing out orders . . . when it first began Te Ropu was very busy and very successful.

But these days I take it easy, producing only a few titles, and most of those chap book size . . . they are easy on the pocket. I now lay the books out on my own computer, and send either disks or hard copies to the printers who do all the rest. Distribution is still a hassle. But the great gain in being a small press publisher is the circle of acquaintances you make.

Over-all the publishing business has more than paid for itself, especially taking also into account the annual Author's Fund grant of over $1000. The book I really got burned on was ***Kaspar's Journey***, for which Brick Row wanted a glossy production which cost the earth. I was thousands of dollars out of pocket over that one. But most titles either cover costs or make a profit.

9 - Where do you place yourself and your achievements as a publisher (and as a writer if applicable) in the history of the modern-day New Zealand literary scene? Do you feel that your contribution has been adequately acknowledged.

On the literary side of my publication I have to rate mine as a very minor contribution to NZ literature since only 25 of my works plus two issues of a magazine are on the list and of those I am Author, co-author or editor of 20! Nevertheless, some of these are quite notable additions to NZ literature: E. Espinoza's bi-lingual poetry collection **shadow-patches** - the first international collection of Haibun in the world - Atihana Johns' short stories, M.K. Joseph's novel. Other productions have also been interesting or even pioneering contributions; **Catching the Light, Other Voices-1**. I think the best of my own work also make their little contribution to the diversity of NZ literature: **Laya**, the first novel set in the Lapita age, **Dare Not Fail**, the first novel for teenagers or maybe the first novel of any sort set among the ancient Moriori, **Blood of Tainui**, and the story collection **Just Like You Said It Would Be**.

I think that Hallard Press has sustained a distinctive voice of dissent or social criticism, one of the very few publishers small or large to do so. My view is that the NZ of the 1990's and 2000's needs that sort of publishing far more than it needs more works of the glitterati.

No, these contributions are little acknowledged among the Glitterati but are acknowledged elsewhere. **The Oxford Companion to NZ Literature** mentions Te Ropu Kahurangi. The Oxford and Penguin literary histories ignore me and my publishing altogether. Who cares? But what does make me mad is when bibliographies fail to acknowledge my presses when we were the first or an earlier publication. I think one problem is the sheer ignorance of some NZ academics.

But acknowledgement is not so much the problem as the immense difficulty of gaining any publicity for publications in newspapers or magazines, even **Landfall**. I do not want to pay out the amounts needed to buy advertising . . . which may not work anyway. Nevertheless, most of the works listed here have eventually gone out of print.

B.G. Auckland, 2000.

Publisher: Hard Echo Press.

Warwick Sven Jordan, printer and poet who published a variety of New Zealand poets and authors in the 1980's. Initially he used the imprint Royal Frog Publications (later RF), changing to Hard Echo around 1983. In recent times Warwick has become involved in setting up a chain of good quality second-hand bookshops, the principal one being Hard To Find Bookshop in Onehunga.

As Royal Frog Publications

JORDAN, Warwick, *My Canary Drinks Meths*, 1980, Poetry and illustrations (100 copies)

JORDAN, Warwick, *Arnold the Frog Meets Proteus*, 1981, Poetry (300 copies)

JORDAN, Warwick, *Selection of Poems on a Single Sheet*, 1981, Poetry (800 copies)

JORDAN, Warwick, *Inserts*, 1983, Poetry, illustrated by Julia Royackers (300 copies)

LEES, Susan, et al, *Words: angry, mystical and melancholic*, 1981, Poetry, with Warwick Jordan, and Sandra (Bronwyn Fark a.k.a. Liz Fear)

LEES, Susan, et al, *A Selection of Poems*, 1982, Poetry, with Warwick Jordan and Bronwyn Fark (100 copies)

LEES, Susan, *A Ceiling for a Sky*, 1982, Poetry (300 copies)

As Hard Echo Press

BARFORD, Cherie, ***A Plea to the Spanish Lady***, 1985, Poetry (300 copies)

BARFORD, Cherie, ***Glass Canisters***, 1989, Poetry (300 copies)

BEYER, Tony, ***Brute Music***, 1984, Poetry (300 copies)

CONNELL, Maurice, ***Origins***, 1986, Poetry (300 copies)

HOWARD, David, ***Head First***, 1985, Poetry (300 copies)

JOHNSON, Mike, ***From a Woman in Mt. Eden Prison and Drawing Lessons***, 1984, Poetry (100 copies)

JOHNSON, Mike, ***Standing Wave***, 1985, Poetry (300 copies)

JOHNSON, Mike, ***Lear***, 1986, Novel (1000 copies)

JOHNSON, Mike, ***Anti-Body Positive***, 1988, Novel (1500 copies)

JOHNSON, Mike, ***Lethal Dose***, 1991, Novel (2000 copies)

JOHNSON, Stephanie, ***The Bleeding Ballerina***, 1987, Poetry (300 copies)

JORDAN, Warwick, ***Tuatara***, 1983, Poetry (10 copies)

JORDAN, Warwick, et al, ***Freewords***, 1984, Poetry, with Susan Lees and Rosie Scott (1000 copies)

JORDAN, Warwick, ***Razors on the Slide***, 1984 , Poetry, (300 copies) reprint (300)

JORDAN, Warwick, ***Borrowed Time***, 1986, Poetry, includes a short prose work by Boris Webb, (300) reprint (300)

JORDAN, Warwick, ***Three Brothers***, 1986, Poetry (120 copies)

LEES, Susan, ***Grandmother***, 1984, Poetry (100 copies)

LEES, Susan, ***Adder's Tongue***, 1984 1985, Poetry, (300 copies) reprint (300)

MENZIES, Rosemary, ed., ***The Globe Tapes***, 1985, Poetry, book and tape set, 42 N.Z. poets read their work (300)

MURPHY, Brian, ***Inside! (Wi Tako Prison)***, 1983, Poetry (100 copies)

NORCLIFFE, James, ***The Sportsman and Other Poems: Rites of Admission,*** 1987, Poetry (300 copies)

PATERSON, Mike, ***Goodstuff any Moment***, 1987, Novel (1000 copies)

RICHARDSON, Paddy, ***Choices***, 1986, Short stories (300 copies)

SCOTT, Rosie, ***Flesh and Blood***, 1984, Poetry (300 copies)

SHARP, Iain, ***She's Trying to Kidnap the Blind Person***, 1985, Poetry (300 copies)

SHARP, Iain, ***The Pierrot Variations***, 1985, Poetry (300 copies)

1 - What was your initial reason for getting involved in publishing ? Please try to think of this in the spirit of what you were thinking and doing at the time.

Enthusiasm for literature in general and a desire to be involved in it. Along with that, spirit didn't have a lot to do with it - whiskey mainly! A desire to do things "my way", on my terms. The only real compromise I made on that was letting George Stockman influence me. He pushed me into getting serious about it in the late 80's - and occasionally still harasses me about getting back into it (always a possibility I suppose).

2 - Who or what was your main influence behind your decision to publish? These may include literary or non-literary influences.

Mostly O'Ban, but also Jack Daniels and Absolut. Lengthy conversations with George Stockman about leading an interesting life. Something to do when my motorbike was getting fixed.

3 - In your choice of authors was the main consideration for inclusion philosophical, literary or pragmatic?

Literary, and a desire to get away from parochial New Zealand writing.

4 - ". . . and if there is still a number of commissioned works which seemed to have been dreamed up by a sabotaging office boy on an LSD trip, there are now each year a growing quantity of books which worthily add to our literature." - Professor J.C. Reid from an article introducing *New Zealand Books in Print*, written in 1968. I interpret Reid's assessment as an indication of the rift between the acceptable, 'worthy' literature as endorsed by academia, and the new wave of sabotaging office boys and girls who at that time commissioned publishers to put out their works, or simply published things themselves and in many cases the works of their friends. Comment on this quote in relation to the 'Vanity Press' vs 'Real Publishing' debate.

Wasn't an issue for me. Apart from my own stuff authors did not contribute any publishing costs and therefor it was not vanity press work. I printed books for a few people for money but not under the Hard Echo imprint.

I wanted to have total editorial control and maintain a standard which George and I established. I also wanted to treat my authors like professional writers, I wanted to assist them and promote them in every way. I'm still proud of the standard and writing I published (excluding most of my own crap).

5 - Initially, was your focus outwardly cosmopolitan or inwardly New Zealand looking, and how has this emphasis changed over the years?

Outwardly cosmopolitan. It didn't change.

6 - What were your methods of printing and distribution as a publisher? Did you receive any financial or other assistance from either public organizations, or private sponsorship?

I taught myself how to print as I found printing too poor a quality or too expensive for my non-existent budget. I bought the gear and figured it out. ***Tuatara*** (HEP's first publication) was originally printed without a printing press (I just stood on it).

I got grants from the Literary Fund to help reduce retail prices, and a one-off grant to assist my financial situation. I also got an Arts Council grant for handcraft printing (the only one at the time). Ironically, printing was a means to an end for me, I never produced anything of superior printing quality. I tried to get private sponsorship, but lacked the profile companies want to get advertising rewards from.

I tried professional distributors, but they weren't much help. Distribution was the big problem for a small press, a lot of it was door-knocking at shops run by morons.

7 - How much of your publishing was commissioned and paid for (either fully or partially) by the author? Was your

operation helped by the voluntary work of friends and family?

(a) None.

(b) on a couple of large publications friends and family helped with collation. My mother lent me money for my first press, then gave up hope of ever getting paid back.

8 - What has been the cost to you personally in terms of time, money and resources of being involved in publishing in New Zealand? You may consider this in relation to more difficult areas such as relationships with friends, family etc.

It took a lot of time, money and resources. It was often hard work and long hours with little or no gratitude or glory. I stopped publishing because I realised that my efforts were not appreciated and that some of the authors I dealt with were mercenaries who saw me as part of the "publisher" establishment out to do authors out of their rightful gains. I lost tens of thousands of dollars helping to launch the careers of others. Thanks of any sort were in short supply and I lost heart.

9 - Where do you place yourself and your achievements as a publisher (and as a writer if applicable) in the history of the modern day New Zealand literary scene? Do you feel that your contribution has been adequately acknowledged?

In the modern day literary scene I helped launch a number of now established writers - authors (e.g.. Rosie Scott, Mike Johnson, Stephanie Johnson, David Howard, James Norcliffe, Iain Sharp). Most of them are mentioned in the various literary surveys (***Oxford History of New Zealand Literature*** etc. etc.) - I'm not.

W.S.J. Northland, 2000.

--- --- ---

Publisher: Hawk Press.

Alan Loney, perhaps one of the most influential and enigmatic characters in New Zealand literature in the last thirty years. Loney sought to marry innovative poetic style with aesthetic craftsmanship, making the finished book a work of art as well as literature.

BEAGLEHOLE, J.C., ***The Death of Captain Cook***, 1979, Scholarship, for the Alexander Turnbull Library

BEAGLEHOLE, J.C., ***The New Zealand Scholar***, 1982, Scholarship (100 copies)

BRUNTON, Alan, ***Black and White Anthology***, 1976, Poetry (300 copies)

BURTON, P. , ***Orange's Skins are Free***, Poetry, with photographs by Warwick Smith (200 copies)

CREELEY, Robert, ***Hello***, Poetry (750 copies)

DONOVAN, Anne, ***Daddy Am I So Fine***, 1978, Poetry (300 copies)

EDMOND, Murray, ***Patchwork***, Poetry, with monoprints by Janet Paul (300 copies)

FAUST, Clive, ***Metamorphosed from the Adjacent Cold***, Poetry (200 copies)

HALEY, Russell, ***The Balkan Transformer (Hawkeye 2)***, 1977, Short story, pamphlet (300 copies)

HALEY, Russell, ***On the Fault Line and Other Poems***, 1977, Poetry (300 copies)

HARLOW, Michael, ***Texts, Identities (Hawkeye 3)***, 1978, Poetry, pamphlet (300 copies)

HARRISON, Martin, ***Truce***, 1979, Poetry (200 copies)

HORROCKS, Roger, ***Auckland Regional Transit Poetry Line***, 1982, Poetry, co-published with Brick Row Publishing

JENNER, Ted, ***A Memorial Brass***, 1980, Poetry (200 copies)

LINDSAY, Graham, ***Thousand-Eyed Eel***, 1976, A sequence of poems from the Māori Land March, 1975 (300 copies)

LONEY, Alan, ***dear Mondrian***, 1976, Poetry, with drawings by Robin Neate (300 copies)

LONEY, Alan, ***Squeezing the Bones***, 1983, Poetry and prints (15 copies)

MANHIRE, Bill, ***Dawn/Water***, 1979, Text by Bill Manhire; images by Andrew Drummond (200 copies)

MANSFIELD, Edgar, ***11.2.80 : On Creation*** (150 copies)

MILLER, David, ***Appearance & Event***, 1977, 16 Poems (300 copies)

OLIVER, Stephen, ***Henwise***, 1975, A poem sequence, cover drawing by Polly Barr (300 copies)

ORR, Bob, ***Poems for Moira***, 1979, Poetry (200 copies)

PASLEY, Rhys, ***Cafe Life & The Train***, 1977, Two poems

PAUL, Joanna, ***Imogen***, 1978, Poetry (300 copies)

SCOTT, L.E., ***This Bitter Earth (Hawkeye 4)***, 1978, Poetry, pamphlet (300 copies)

SMITHER, Elizabeth, ***The Sarah Train***, 1980, Poetry (300 copies)

WEDDE, Ian, ***Don't Listen (Hawkeye 1)***, 1977, Poetry, pamphlet (500 copies)

WEDDE, Ian, ***Pathway to the Sea***, 1975, Poetry (300 copies)

As Black Light Press

CURNOW, Wystan, ***Back in the USA: poems 1980 - 82***, 1989, Poetry (300 copies)

LONEY, Alan, ***Ampersand***, 1990, Printing history (150 copies)

MALE, John, ***Poems from a War***, 1989, Poetry, limited ed. with 8 drawings by Russell Clark, foreword by Guy Powles (33 copies)

SIMPSON, Tony, ***Cargo of Flux: an Incident from Early New Zealand***, 1991, Māori history, limited, signed ed. (50 copies)

1 - What was your initial reason for getting involved in publishing? Please try to think of this in the spirit of what you were thinking and doing at the time.

I felt that there was worthwhile poetry being written that was not getting published, and that books that were being published could be better designed and produced than was the case at the time.

But it was also the case that new poetry, heralded by the appearance of **FREED** magazine, (1969 - 1972) was, in my view then (and I believe now in the year 2000 that this view was correct) not only not being adequately presented in the mainstream, but was being resisted. Appallingly, this situation has not changed today, in spite of the considerable documentable achievements of most of those who were part of the new poetry.

2 - Who or what was your main influence behind your decision to publish? These may include literary or non-literary influences.

See question 1

3 - In your choice of authors was the main consideration for inclusion philosophical, literary or pragmatic?

See question 1

4 - "...and if there is still a number of commissioned works which seem to have been dreamed up by a sabotaging office-boy on an LSD trip, there are now each year a growing quantity of books which worthily add to our literature." Professor J.C. Reid from an article introducing *New Zealand Books in Print*, written in 1968. I interpret Reid's assessment as an indication of the rift between the acceptable 'worthy' literature as endorsed by academia, and the new wave of sabotaging office boys and girls who at that time commissioned publishers to put out their works, or simply published things themselves, and in many cases the work of their friends. Comment on this quote in relation to the 'Vanity Press' vs 'Real Publishing' debate.

This question, and its kind, are of no interest or relevance to me.

5 - Initially, was your focus outwardly cosmopolitan or inwardly New Zealand looking, and how has this emphasis changed over the years?

From the beginning I understood that New Zealand poetry took place in an international context. It did in the 1930's when the canon was newly formed (then the new poets were British); and it did again in the 1970's when the established canon was challenged (then the new poets were European and American). I did in fact publish four books by overseas writers.

6 - What were your methods of printing and distribution as a publisher? Did you receive any financial or other assistance from either public organisations, or private sponsorship?

The press's production was letterpress, with handset metal type, hand printing and hand sewing and binding. Distribution was direct from the press, except for its last year or so, when distribution was by Brick Row Publishing Co.

My policy was that I'd avoid applying for Literary Fund / Arts Council grants for specific books, the concern being not wanting to get reliant on them.

However, got one grant for buying type from overseas, and another for experimenting with multi-colour printing - but these were not publishing grants.

Else, one person gave me $1000 as forward payment on books to come. That person will remain anonymous.

7 - How much of your publishing was commissioned and paid for (either fully or partially) by the author? Was your operation helped by the voluntary work of friends and family?

No authors paid for their books to be published. When I lived with Alison Tetley in the early 1980's she was involved in the press for about 2 years. Else, it was always a one-person event.

8 - What has been the cost to you personally in terms of time, money and resources, of being involved in

publishing in New Zealand? You may consider this in relation to more difficult areas such as relationships with friends, family etc. also.

I never made money from my years as a printer / publisher. In the later life of Hawk Press, it utterly depended [sic] on the fact that my partner worked as a teacher.

What it cost finally was any chance of owning a house or looking after my life after 'retirement'. It has, I have to say, been of some regret that my chosen career was never going to provide me with a level of financial security - of a kind for instance that is provided to many whose contribution to the literary scene is so much less than one's own.

9 - Where do you place yourself and your achievements as a publisher (and as a writer if applicable) in the history of the modern-day New Zealand literary scene? Do you feel that your contribution has been adequately acknowledged.

I cannot answer the first question. Nor, really, the second, except to say that almost no contributors to "the other tradition" in New Zealand have been adequately acknowledged, and that it is usual, when noticed at all, to be noticed in negative, even punitive terms, by writers who have shown no interest in the history or the context of that tradition.

A.L. Christchurch, 2000.

Publisher: HeadworX.

Mark Pirie is a writer and editor who has made an impact in recent years with his publication of stylish poetry volumes by poets often neglected by the literary establishment. In his ground-breaking anthology *The NeXt Wave* he explored the concerns of 'Generation X' through their writings, poetry and song lyrics. He is also editor of *JAAM*.

BERNHARDT, Jeanne Catrin, ***Baby is this wonderland?***, 1999, Prose, cover art by the author (150 copies)

BEYER, Tony, ***The Century***, 1998, Poetry, cover art by Russell Chalmers (150 copies)

ENSING, Riemke, ***Talking Pictures: Selected Poems***, 2000, Poetry, cover art by Judith Haswell (600 copies)

McQUEEN, Harvey, ***Pingandy: New & Selected Poems***, 1999, Poetry, cover art by Russell Chalmers (250 copies)

OLIVER, Stephen, ***Unmanned***, 1999, Poetry, over art by Margaret-Ann Hamilton (500 copies)

PLUMB, Vivienne, ***Salamanca***, 1998, Poetry, designed by Mark Pirie (210 copies)

PLUMB, Vivienne, ***The diary as a positive in female adult behaviour,*** 1999, Fiction, cover art by Russell Chalmers (250 copies)

POWELL -CHALMERS, Jenny, ***Sweet banana wax peppers***, 1998, Poetry, cover art by Russell Chalmers (210 copies)

POWELL - CHALMERS, Jenny, ***Hats***, 2000, Poetry (500 copies)

RICKETTS, Harry, ***Nothing to Declare: selected writings 1977 - 1997***, 1998, Poetry, and fiction with book design by Mark Pirie (300 copies)

SCOTT, L.E., *Earth Colours: Selected Poems*, 2000, Poetry, cover art by Russell Chalmers (500 copies)

1 - What was your initial reason for getting involved in publishing? Please try to think of this in the spirit of what you were thinking and doing at the time.

My initial reason to get involved in publishing was due to my own personal interest in publishing. I always wanted to be involved in publishing in some form and after finishing Honours at Victoria in 1997 I started HeadworX to gain further hands-on experience which would eventually lead to further jobs in editing/publishing. I also liked the idea of publishing work and helping authors get their work in print, and especially liked the idea of providing a publishing alternative outside of the academic coteries that have developed in recent years. I thought their elitist/selective approach to literature as shown in the Histories/Companions/Oxford Poetry anthologies was damaging to the full range and long-term development of literature in New Zealand. In my view Terry Locke's secondary school anthologies just released (see *Doors* and *Jewels in the Water,* Leaders Press, 2000) are far more representative than the OUP one in 1997. *Big Smoke* (AUP, 2000) is also good in terms of representing a wider range of poets.

2 - Who or what was your main influence behind your decision to publish? These may include literary or non-literary influences.

I didn't really have any literary influences as such I was just willing to publish whatever good manuscripts I could find or whatever was sent to me. The majority of work I have solicited and put together myself, e.g. Harry Ricketts, Jenny Powell-Chalmers, Harvey McQueen, Riemke Ensing, L.E.Scott. Stephen Oliver, Jeanne Bernhardt and Vivienne Plumb were all submitted to me. But I did have a few influences in mind. For instance Louis Johnson, who I always admired for his heroic attempts to get as many authors in print as possible and for his work in breaking down the academic coteries and selective approach to literature through his ***Poetry Yearbooks*** (1951 - 64). Other influences in publishing were New Directions and Black Sparrow Press and Faber and Faber, in terms of book design, typesetting, etc. I was interested in a stylish format and I rifled through as many poetry books in the library to study how the books had been put together. I also had the good fortune of meeting Russell Chalmers, the husband of Jenny Powell-Chalmers, who contributed excellent covers for most of the books.

3 - In your choice of authors was the main consideration for inclusion philosophical, literary or pragmatic?

My main choice for inclusion was that the work was of 'good' literary merit, or so it seemed to me - reviewers may see it differently of course! Other than that some of the authors I have published have tended to be 'outsiders' in the literary community, some have been neglected authors who haven't been properly recognized for their work, and some have been new authors who have found it difficult to get their manuscripts published because they weren't established as a 'name' author. So HeadworX has filled a gap in the market by allowing these authors to get in print whereas the established commercial presses might not have published them due to either financial reasons or personal prejudice and dislike of their particular writing style.

4 - "...and if there is still a number of commissioned works which seem to have been dreamed up by a sabotaging office-boy on an LSD trip, there are now each year a growing quantity of books which worthily add to our literature." Professor J.C. Reid from an article introducing *New Zealand Books in Print*, written in 1968. I interpret Reid's assessment as an indication of the rift between the acceptable 'worthy' literature as endorsed by academia, and the new wave of sabotaging office boys and girls who at that time commissioned publishers to

put out their works, or simply published things themselves, and in many cases the work of their friends. Comment on this quote in relation to the 'Vanity Press' vs 'Real Publishing' debate.

No comment.

5 - Initially, was your focus outwardly cosmopolitan or inwardly New Zealand looking, and how has this emphasis changed over the years?

HeadworX has been Australasian in focus. I'm interested in publishing both Australian and New Zealand authors, but my editing of the literary magazine *JAAM* has been very international in outlook. We have published authors from Malaysia, Thailand, Australia, the US, Brazil, Canada etc. I think this international, cosmopolitan flavour has certainly changed over the years and New Zealand authors are now confident to see their work alongside the best of overseas poetry.

6 - What were your methods of printing and distribution as a publisher? Did you receive any financial or other assistance from either public organisations, or private sponsorship?

I have used low-run docu-tech digital printing at Massey and Otago Printeries. This is high speed 'photocopying' but the finish is very good. I have some financial assistance from Creative New Zealand. 3 of the 10 books I've published have been funded. The amounts have varied, however. I only received $500 to publish Harvey McQueen's work, which doesn't even help to cover the printing costs of such a book. I started out distributing the books myself by going around the bookshops and placing them on sale or return but now I prefer to use a distributor as it removes the personal burden to me in this respect. My books are distributed in New Zealand and Australia by reputable distributors: Nationwide in Christchurch and

Dennis Jones in Melbourne. *Note:* I have recently switched to Addenda in Auckland for local distribution.

7 - How much of your publishing was commissioned and paid for (either fully or partially) by the author? Was your operation helped by the voluntary work of friends and family?

I have paid for the cost of publishing myself mostly. But I have accepted money from the authors in terms of selling them 40 or 50 copies at wholesale discount on publication to recoup my costs. These copies were then used for personal sale by the authors to friends and at readings and events. My operation was helped by voluntary work from the authors in terms of readings and marketing and by designers such as Russell Chalmers and Judith Haswell. All the typesetting, book promotion, advertising, editing and book design has been done by me.

8 - What has been the cost to you personally in terms of time, money and resources, of being involved in publishing in New Zealand? You may consider this in relation to more difficult areas such as relationships with friends, family etc. also.

The cost has been enormous. To the extent that it cost me a social life. The amount of time consumed by these activities is something I'm looking at as I will probably look to publish only 4 titles a year maximum. It has left me financially broke most of the time as well. This is something that doesn't trouble me too much at this stage but in the future if I do settle down and raise a family, publishing may have to go. However, now that I'm [working] full-time the financial burden has been lifted somewhat, so who knows? I will probably stick at it.

9 - Where do you place yourself and your achievements as a publisher (and as a writer if applicable) in the history

of the modern-day New Zealand literary scene? Do you feel that your contribution has been adequately acknowledged.

I'd like to think I have done good work in opening up the New Zealand literary scene a little and letting more voices become accepted here. I'm simply following on the good work that's been done by the likes of Louis Johnson. I don't make any claim to exerting an influence on people's writing styles or instigating a particular direction. I suppose though my anthology ***The NeXt Wave*** was an attempt to sum up a particular generation's writing style and way of saying but it has been misrepresented in some ways and has suffered the brunt of coterie attacks. The book to me was more concerned with including a wider range of writing styles than would be normally acceptable to the established presses. For instance rhyming verse and song lyrics feature alongside more obscure postmodern academic styles. Interestingly I have since received quite a lot of acclaim overseas from critics in India and the US. A favourable review was published in ***World Literature Today*** (June 1999). So I would say local critics have underestimated me and this is partly due to the coterie backlash I have received from the book. At the moment I will just keep going on the direction I have already charted for myself and keep up the good work. Acclaim is not really of vital importance though it is nice to receive some recognition for one's efforts, and this is already coming in dribs and drabs, both overseas and locally. My support is growing. What more can one ask for?

M.P. Wellington, 2000.

Publisher: Huia Publishing.

Robyn Bargh began as a publisher of Māori literary writings and Huia have become the major publisher of Māori literary and educational works and textbooks, with a kaupapa to further the advancement of Māori literature in New Zealand Aotearoa, and internationally.

GARLICK, Jennifer, ***Maori Language Publishing***, 1998, Some issues involving publishing Te Reo Māori

GRACE, Patricia, ***I Retireti Atu Au***, 1996, Nga korero, with Kerehi Waiariki. Illustrated by Kerry Gemmill

GRACE-SMITH, Briar, ***Nga Pou Wahine***, 1997, Playscript

GRACE-SMITH, Briar, ***Purapurawhetu***, 1999, Playscript

IHIMAERA, Witi, ***Woman Far Walking***, 2000, Playscript

KAWANA, Phil, ***Attack of the Skunk People***, 1999, Fiction

KAWANA, Phil, ***Dead Jazz Guys: and Other Stories***, 1996, Fiction

KOUKA, Hone, ***Waiora: te Ukaipo***, 1997, Playscript, with waiata by Hone Hurihanganui

ROYAL, Charles, ed., ***Kati Au i Konei***, 1994, A collection of songs from Ngati Toarangatira and Ngati Raukawa

TAYLOR, Apirana, ***He Tangi Aroha***, 1993, Novel

THORNTON, Agathe, ***Maori Oral Literature***, 1999, As seen by a classicist

Huia Short Stories: 1,2 & 3, 1995 1997 1999, Collections of short stories from the Huia authors

YOUNG, David, ***Woven by Water***, 1998, Histories from the Whanganui River

YOUNG, Hepora, ***Hinemoa & Tutanekai***, 1995, A Te Arawa legend retold with illustrations by Kerry Gemmill

1 - What was your initial reason for getting involved in publishing? Please try to think of this in the spirit of what you were thinking and doing at the time.

I set up Huia Publishers in 1991 because I considered that New Zealand literature did not adequately represent the views, values and attitudes of Māori people I knew. I really enjoy reading literature of other indigenous people and I felt we could have a much better expression of a much more diverse New Zealand. This expanded into the publishing of educational materials in Māori.

2 - Who or what was your main influence behind your decision to publish? These may include literary or non-literary influences.

Literary influences from other countries included Alice Walker, Maya Angelou, Toni Morrison, Sherma Alexie, Richard Wright, Gabriel Garcia Marquez, Ben Oki, Salmon Rushdie, Dale Spender, Dee Brown, etc.

Non-literary influences were the many Māori people I grew up with & know who have interesting ideas & lives & who can view the world in different ways.

3 - In your choice of authors was the main consideration for inclusion philosophical, literary or pragmatic?

At Huia the main consideration for the development of the list is philosophical. The works have to contribute in some way to the development of Māori writers or literary thought.

4 - "...and if there is still a number of commissioned works which seem to have been dreamed up by a sabotaging office-boy on an LSD trip, there are now each year a growing quantity of books which worthily add to our literature." Professor J.C. Reid from an article introducing *New Zealand Books in Print*, written in 1968. I interpret Reid's assessment as an indication of the rift between the acceptable 'worthy' literature as endorsed by academia, and the new wave of sabotaging office boys and girls who at that time commissioned publishers to put out their works, or simply published things themselves, and in many cases the work of their friends. Comment on this quote in relation to the 'Vanity Press' vs 'Real Publishing' debate.

I don't see the work of Huia Publishers as vanity publishing, but nor is it the 'worthy' type endorsed by academia. Huia Publishers is working to extend the boundaries of NZ literature.

5 - Initially, was your focus outwardly cosmopolitan or inwardly New Zealand looking, and how has this emphasis changed over the years?

We are wanting to reflect on Māori experiences in a way that the rest of the world will want to read.

6 - What were your methods of printing and distribution as a publisher? Did you receive any financial or other assistance from either public organisations, or private sponsorship?

Most of our books are subsidised, either by funds from private or public organisations, or by Huia Publishers funds.

Huia staff organize all aspects of production - design, typesetting, printing, promotion and distribution.

7 - How much of your publishing was commissioned and paid for (either fully or partially) by the author? Was your operation helped by the voluntary work of friends and family?

See previous page.

8 - What has been the cost to you personally in terms of time, money and resources, of being involved in publishing in New Zealand? You may consider this in relation to more difficult areas such as relationships with friends, family etc. also.

I have been involved in publishing since 1991. It takes over 60 hours a week and much money & other resources. However, I still thoroughly enjoy my work & can't imagine doing anything else. Much of my family is also involved - either full-time, part-time or in a support role.

9 - Where do you place yourself and your achievements as a publisher (and as a writer if applicable) in the history of the modern-day New Zealand literary scene? Do you feel that your contribution has been adequately acknowledged.

It is a bit too early to consider this & I am not the best person to ask. Ask Māori people in 50 years time.

R.B. Wellington, 2000.

Publisher: Miracle Mart Receiving.

Gregory O'Brien, a poet, novelist and painter who has experimented with various forms of alternative publishing, often in collaboration with others. Also includes: Modern House, Wellington Plains, Keretene Press, Animated Figure, "Brendan O'Brien," "Jack O'Brien."

Miracle Mart Receiving (see Journals)

Modern House with Anne Kennedy

O'BRIEN, Gregory, ***Dunes and Barns***, 1988, Poetry (300 copies)

SMITHER, Elizabeth & McKENNA, Noel, ***Animaux***, 1988, Poetry (250 copies)

von STURMER, Richard, ***We Xerox Your Zebras***, 1988, Poetry (500 copies)

Wellington Plains

O'BRIEN, Gregory, ***Malachi***, 1990, Poetry, limited edition (20 copies)

Keretene Press

O'BRIEN, Gregory, ***In Rain (INRI)***, 1990, Poetry, hand-printed edition (22 copies)

O'BRIEN, Gregory, ***Five Poems***, 1990, Poetry (6 copies)

Animated Figure

O'BRIEN, Gregory, ***The Time and How***, 1996, Poetry (77 copies)

O'BRIEN, Gregory, ***Talking Toss Woollaston***, 1996, Interview with the artist (11 copies)

O'BRIEN, Gregory, ***Seven Letters***, 1997, Poetry (36 copies)

O'BRIEN, Gregory, ***Caravan***, 1997, Poetry, with Jenny Bornholdt and Noel McKenna (75 copies)

O'BRIEN, Gregory, ***Spinet (for Federico Mompou)***, 1998, Poetry, (15 copies) photocopied second ed., (revised) (13 copies)

O'BRIEN, Gregory, ***A Ride Through the Disturbed Districts of New Zealand: three sequences of poems from Oct. 1983 to Sept. 1984,*** 1998, Photocopied edition (22 copies)

"Brendan O'Brien"

BORNHOLDT, Jenny, ***27.12.96 / Six Poem for Bill Manhire***, 1996, Poetry, handprinted edition with Dinah Hawken, Andrew Johnston, Bill Manhire, Gregory O'Brien, Chris Orsman and Damien Wilkins (35 copies)

MANHIRE, Bill, ***Moonlight***, 1996, Poetry, handprinted, signed edition (35 copies)

O'BRIEN, Gregory, ***A Small Book of Paintings by Milton Avery***, 1999, Poetry, handprinted, signed edition (23 copies)

"Jack O'Brien"

O'BRIEN, Jack, ***Visiting the Ralph Hotere Exhibition with Ross Stevens, June 5***, 1998, Memoir, handprinted (4 copies)

In conjunction with Wai-te-ata Press, Wellington

BORNHOLDT, Jenny, ***These Things***, 1999, Poetry, handprinted, signed edition illustrated by Gregory O'Brien (100 copies)

Miracle Mart Receiving*

Journals

O'BRIEN, Gregory, ed., ***Rambling Jack, Nos. 1 - 5***, 1986 1987, Literary magazine, (500 - 600 copies per issue)

*Miracle Mart Receiving was taken over in 1987 by E.S.A.W. (see E.S.A.W. bibliography).

1 - What was your initial reason for getting involved in publishing? Please try to think of this in the spirit of what you were thinking and doing at the time.

I've always considered "alternative" forms of publishing as being a central and integral part of the literary culture: a complement as well as an antidote to mainstream publishing. My heroes in this respect were:

Jonathon Williams & his Jargon Press
(Dent Dale & North Carolina)
Alan Loney & his Hawk Press
James Langhlin & New Directions (in the early days)
Ken Bolton (Adelaide)
John Forbes (Sydney)

I like to be able to produce things quickly & without pandering to market forces. Also, commercial publishers will not publish booklets or small-scale literary works. A piece of work of 24pp is just as valid as one of, say, 172pp. It's important for works to be presented intact, as 'works'. So you get books like ***DUNES & BARNS***.

2 - Who or what was your main influence behind your decision to publish? These may include literary or non-literary influences.

See Q.1. As someone who has worked as a visual artist, I like the handmade art-object rather than the mass-produced 'product'. The small books I have produced have often been distributed at gallery openings - they are an integral part of my work as a visual artist as well as a writer. The fact my father, Jack, & my brother Brendan both have letterpress printing devices has obviously bolstered my enthusiasm for such modes of production.

3 - In your choice of authors was the main consideration for inclusion philosophical, literary or pragmatic?

Pragmatic.

I have published quite a lot of my own work because I have wanted to circulate it among friends. There's a satisfaction in by-passing the time-consuming & often distracting aspects of more conventional publication.

Also:

Certain texts require certain types of "publishing": - small fragmentary works (***THE TIME & HOW, IRISHMAN & INDUSTRY*** (Pear Tree Press), & ***A SMALL BOOK OF PAINTINGS*** . . .) are best done in small handpress editions.

At other times a pile of stapled A4 paper seems most appropriate (e.g.. ***SPINET, A RIDE THROUGH THE DISTURBED REGIONS***).

The writing is what counts NOT the imprint, the distributor, the literary world. Review copies of my recent books are never sent out - there is no ISBN number - the books are free to exist on their own anarchic, independent terms.

4 - "...and if there is still a number of commissioned works which seem to have been dreamed up by a sabotaging office-boy on an LSD trip, there are now each year a growing quantity of books which worthily add to our literature." Professor J.C. Reid from an article introducing *New Zealand Books in Print*, written in 1968. I interpret Reid's assessment as an indication of the rift between the acceptable 'worthy' literature as endorsed by academia, and the new wave of sabotaging office boys and girls who at that time commissioned publishers to put out their works, or simply published things them-

selves, and in many cases the work of their friends. Comment on this quote in relation to the 'Vanity Press' vs 'Real Publishing' debate.

I don't think there is any distinction: - the 'bad boy' Eggleton was published by Penguin - the 'independent' Loney by AUP.

The work moves around, as it should. A flexible publishing climate is ideal. And because there is no money in poetry publishing, generally poets aren't contractually bound to a single outlet.

Long live variousness, unruly-ness.

5 - Initially, was your focus outwardly cosmopolitan or inwardly New Zealand looking, and how has this emphasis changed over the years?

Writing is all that matters, no matter where. In the late 1980's & early 1990's I published far more material in Australia than in New Zealand. The writing exists wherever it is being read, not only where it was written. My most NZ flavoured book, ***DAYS BESIDE WATER***, was published by Carcanet in the UK. What does this mean? Maybe poetry needs to be outward as well as inward looking & in perpetual motion. The emphasis is always changing.

6 - What were your methods of printing and distribution as a publisher? Did you receive any financial or other assistance from either public organisations, or private sponsorship?

RAMBLING JACK a little arts council money (between $300 & $500 per edition from memory) ***WE XEROX YOUR ZEBRAS*** received a small Lit. Fund grant. Everything else is self-financed or produced in return for art works etc.

7 - How much of your publishing was commissioned and paid for (either fully or partially) by the author? Was your

operation helped by the voluntary work of friends and family?

The only author to contribute was myself. The good offices of J.B. & J.P. O'Brien have often printed the material.

8 - What has been the cost to you personally in terms of time, money and resources, of being involved in publishing in New Zealand? You may consider this in relation to more difficult areas such as relationships with friends, family etc. also.

I find it hard to 'cost' the time I have spent in the writing & production of these poems / books. They are part of life - they are hard work - they just get done.

The way to survive as a writer is not to rely on other people / publishers / critics but to define your own space . . . 'the favourable furrow and the loving effort of an entire life', as Rovault put it (from memory).

Bitterness or disappointment waste the energy that should be directed towards making new work.

9 - Where do you place yourself and your achievements as a publisher (and as a writer if applicable) in the history of the modern-day New Zealand literary scene? Do you feel that your contribution has been adequately acknowledged.

Again, my job is to make work, not to place it in 'history'.

The work exists, obscurely, funnily.

My friends & family & a few enthusiastic readers acknowledge what's going on. That's the important thing.

G. O'B. Wellington, 2000.

Publisher: Montgomery Publications.

Peter Olds is a poet with a rebellious, rock and roll reputation. He was the first to publish Dunedin poet John Gibb as well as his own early works. Olds is still writing today. The name for his press comes from Montgomery Avenue, a small street which runs beside the Leith River in the university area of Dunedin.

GIBB, John, ***Two Town Poems***, 1973, Poetry (100 copies)

OLDS, Peter, ***Schizophrenic Highway***, 1971, Poetry (400 copies)

OLDS, Peter, ***Two V8 Poems (Psycho, Revisiting V8 Nostalgia)***, 1971, Poetry (300 copies)

OLDS, Peter, ***In Auckland***, 1971, Poetry (300 copies)

OLDS, Peter, ***Two Poems (And now it's Autumn, In the Morning it Rains)***, 1972, Poetry (100 copies)

OLDS, Peter, ***Exit Poems (I have just Dropped, I need to hide)***, 1972, Poetry (100 copies)

Statement about publishing by Peter Olds

Each time a broadsheet came out it was like releasing a 45 rpm single. That same sense of anticipation as an eagerly awaited new record by your favourite artist was felt in the air. And, of course, the publication of a whole book of poems was the equivalent of an L.P. This is how closely rock n' roll was associated with literature for us.

P.O. Dunedin, 2000

Publisher: Nag's Head Press.

Bob Gormack, known throughout literary and book trade circles over a period of many years as a printer of books of fine quality, is also a prolific writer in his own right.

ALLEN, Julia, **Midas Touch**, 1990, Poetry, with illustrations by Kate Bowes (200 copies)

BARRER, Jennifer, **Te Rangianiwaniwa: a Sequence of Poems**, 1988, Poetry (250 copies)

CASELBERG, John, **Lines**, 1989, Scenes and passages from verse dramas, with a valedictory sequence for Colin McCahon (170 copies)

CASELBERG, John, **Matins and Other Verse**, 1992, Poetry

CASELBERG, John, **Six Songs and the Wake**, 1965, Poetry (100 copies)

CASELBERG, John, **Voice of the Maori: a Culture-conflict Anthology**, 1969
    Anthology of prose extracts (200 copies)

CRESSWELL, D'Arcy, **Sonnets: published and from Manuscripts**, 1976, Poetry, selected by Helen Shaw (200 copies)

DIREEN, Bill, **Evolition**, 1995, Poems and lyrics

DIREEN, Bill, **Inklings**, 1988, Poetry (200 copies)

DOWLING, Basil, **Bedlam: a Mid-century Satire**, 1972, Poetry (200 copies)

DOWLING, Basil, **A Little Gallery of Characters**, 1971, Poetry (200 copies)

DOWLING, Basil, ***The Stream: a Reverie of Boyhood***, 1979, Poetry, with illustrations by Graham Oates (200 copies)

DOWLING, Basil, ***The Unreturning Native***, 1973, Poetry (200 copies)

DOWLING, Basil, ***Windfalls and Other Poems***, 1983, Poetry (225 copies)

DUVAL, Terry, ***Clay Pigeons: Fifty Poems of Youth***, 1990, Poetry, with graphics by Errol Shaw (120 copies)

FAIRBURN, A.R.D., ***Slight Misunderstanding***, 1968, Letter, with lino-cuts by Robert Brett (125 copies)

GALLAGHER, Kathleen, ***Gipsy: a Fictional Verse Sequence***, 1993, Poetry, with illustrations by David Nepia (150 copies)

GALLAGHER, Kathleen, ***Tara***, 1987, Poetry (150 copies)

GLOVER, Denis, ***Myself When Young***, 1970, Early verse (150 copies)

GLOVER, Denis, ***To a Particular Woman***, Poetry (300 copies)

GLOVER, Denis, ***To Friends in Russia***, 1979, Poetry (300 copies)

GORMACK, Nick, ***ABC: a Rhyming Alphabet***, 1998, Poetry, with drawings by Jenny Rendall (325 copies)

GORMACK, R.S., ***The Boarding-house***, 1997, A reminiscence in story form (65 copies)

GORMACK, R.S., ***A Christmas Treat; and The Bottle***, 1998, Stories, reminiscent of old Wellington (65 copies)

GORMACK, R.S., ***The Circus***, 1997, A reminiscence in story form (65 copies)

GORMACK, R.S., ***Nag's Head Press***, 1992, An outline history and descriptive checklist of publications to June, 1992 (80 copies)

GORMACK, R.S., ***The Broadsheet***, 1999, Story

HOOPER, Peter, ***Journey Towards an Elegy and Other Poems***, 1969, Poetry (150 copies)

HOWARD, David, ***Holding Company***, 1995, Poetry (150 copies)

MASON, R.A.K., ***R.A.K. Mason at Twenty-five***, 1986, The text of an extended diary-style letter written in the month of the poet's birthday January, 1930 (225 copies)

PAISLEY, John, ***Vigils***, 1985, Poetry, with a memoir by John Caselberg; graphics by Susan Cooke (150 copies)

SHAW, Helen, ***Ambitions of Clouds***, 1981, Poetry (150 copies)

SHAW, Helen, ***Time Told from a Tower***, 1985, Poetry (150 copies)

SOMERVILLE, Dora, ***Maui's Farewell***, 1966, Poetry (150 copies)

SUMMERS, John, ***Hymns E. & O.E.***, Poetry (130 copies)

SUMMERS, John, ***Letters to Joe***, Poetry (300 copies)

WILSON, Patrick, ***At the Window and Other Poems***, 1997, Poetry

1 - What was your initial reason for getting involved in publishing? Please try to think of this in the spirit of what you were thinking and doing at the time.

Literary, literary, literary! (See my ***NHP - an Outline History*** for detailed background, naming etc.)

I was writing from an early age - high school. I read Shakespeare early and went on to Lawrence, Joyce and Proust (in French). A wide reading in English literature and French (Rabelais, Moliere, Stendhal, Flaubert, Baudelaire etc., etc.).

My wartime student diaries (which I published) are jam-packed with literary references.

My ***Centennial History of Barnigo Flat*** is an imaginary literary work conceived in the Spirit of Comedy (after George Meredith - another favourite author).

2 - Who or what was your main influence behind your decision to publish? These may include literary or non-literary influences.

See p.1.

3 - In your choice of authors was the main consideration for inclusion philosophical, literary or pragmatic?

Mainly literary, but also historical reprints and originals.

4 - "...and if there is still a number of commissioned works which seem to have been dreamed up by a sabotaging office-boy on an LSD trip, there are now each year a growing quantity of books which worthily add to our literature." Professor J.C. Reid from an article introducing *New Zealand Books in Print*, written in 1968. I interpret Reid's assessment as an indication of the rift between the acceptable 'worthy' literature as endorsed by academia, and the new wave of sabotaging office boys

and girls who at that time commissioned publishers to put out their works, or simply published things themselves, and in many cases the work of their friends. Comment on this quote in relation to the 'Vanity Press' vs 'Real Publishing' debate.**

No comment.

An odd thing - J.C. Reid was a rare exception in giving some notice to my writing in his anthology ***The Kiwi Laughs*** (1961).

5 - Initially, was your focus outwardly cosmopolitan or inwardly New Zealand looking, and how has this emphasis changed over the years?

Both.

6 - What were your methods of printing and distribution as a publisher? Did you receive any financial or other assistance from either public organisations, or private sponsorship?

Direct mail circulars to libraries, booksellers and standing orders.

7 - How much of your publishing was commissioned and paid for (either fully or partially) by the author? Was your operation helped by the voluntary work of friends and family?

Quite a few commissioned books over the years, nearly all from one Australian publisher who wanted hand-set type both to his own and my design.

Family members have done a lot of sheet folding of book sections.

8 - What has been the cost to you personally in terms of time, money and resources, of being involved in

publishing in New Zealand? You may consider this in relation to more difficult areas such as relationships with friends, family etc. also.

Not much money, lots of time. But a backing interest in typography right from the start. (I worked at Pegasus Press and became a book editor at Whitcome and Tombs i.e. Whitcoulls).

9 - Where do you place yourself and your achievements as a publisher (and as a writer if applicable) in the history of the modern-day New Zealand literary scene? Do you feel that your contribution has been adequately acknowledged.

In 1967 I received an Award for Achievement for printing and writing from the then State Literary Fund. No further state funds or recognition ever received. Not really adequate!

B.G. Christchurch, 2000.

Publisher: One-Eyed Press.

Christodoulos Moisa was a pioneer in the use of photocopying in NZ publishing. Moisa also developed highly aesthetic and artistic elements in his book production. He is a writer and an artist himself and has taught these subjects as well as practiced them. He is currently Head of Art at Kapiti College and lives in Raumati South.

JONES, Wyn, ***Baron Lumbago***, 1987, Poetry, cover by C.E.G. Moisa (600 copies)

KUIPER, Koenraad, ***Mikrokosmos***, 1990, Poetry, illustrated by C.E.G. Moisa (800 copies)

MAHER, John, ***Talking to Johnno***, 1982, Poetry, cover by C.E.G. Moisa, illustrated by Robin Swanney-MacPherson (150 copies)

MOISA, C.E.G., ***Corrigendum***, 1980, Poetry, illustrations by C.E.G. Moisa

MOISA, C.E.G., ***Elegy***, 1987, Poetry, illustrations by C.E.G. Moisa

MOISA, C.E.G., ***Muriwai Motel Sonnets***, 1977, Poetry, cover by C.E.G. Moisa (200 copies)

MOISA, C.E.G., ***Recoil***, 1987, Poetry, collages by C.E.G. Moisa

MOISA, C.E.G., ***Rotlands***, 1987, Poetry, cover by C.E.G. Moisa

MOISA, C.E.G., ***Thirteen or so Poems to Inbetween***, 1987, Poetry, cover by C.E.G. Moisa

OLDS, Peter, ***After Looking for Broadway***, 1985, Poetry, cover by C.E.G. Moisa (1000 copies)

SHARP, Iain, ***Why Mammals Shiver***, 1981, Poetry, illustrated by C.E.G. Moisa (200 copies)

WILLIAMS, Mark, ***Abecedary***, 1973, Poetry, with illustrations by C.E.G. Moisa (200 copies)

1 - What was your initial reason for getting involved in publishing? Please try to think of this in the spirit of what you were thinking and doing at the time.

I had just returned from London where I briefly attended the Sir John Cass School of Art December 1973 after spending eighteen months in Cyprus. I had to leave London because Edward Heath the then British Prime Minister introduced the three day working week to counter the coal miners strike. I was working in a restaurant at night and in the weekends and attending art school during the day. When the working week was reduced I found it hard to keep attending my classes and I returned to N.Z. Taking John Graham's (my painter lecturer) advice when I returned I started work on getting an exhibition of paintings and drawings together. Mark Williams about that time was doing a thesis on Patrick White at Auckland University and was flatting with a young art student that I was going out with. Mark one day said that he would have liked me to illustrate a book of poems that he was hoping to publish. Apparently he came across someone who was running a small press and was keen to get a small edition out. However, it wasn't long before Mark was told that he'd have to pay for this – something like $600 - $1000. I said that I was sure that we could get the book out for less money and volunteered to look into it. I asked around and eventually came up with a plan to try and print the book using an off-set printer and using paper instead of metal plates. There was a fast print place (IMPRINT) down where the bus depot is in down town Auckland where I got a quote for the job. The deal I did with Mark was that I did all the design, illustration, lay-out etc. and that he'd pay for the printing and after we sold the books he'd get his money back and we'd share the profits, if any. This is how ***Abecedary*** came about. By the end of it all I was glad to see it the end of it because I had hand glued all the illustrations and collated the book myself. The black binding tape gave it a professional finish and most people liked it and it was received favourably at the time in ***Craccum***, the Auckland University newspaper. I remember sometime later Tony Green who was Professor of Art History at Auckland University, stopping me in the street and asking me how I went about publishing my books. I outlined the formula and as a result he published a series of small poetry publications using the photocopy method. Later a lot of other poets woke up to the technology and used it to publish their work cheaply . . . and that was the key word, cheap. It was very economical to publish a book using a photocopier and more importantly you had total control over your own work. Later of course with help from the QEII Arts Council I published several books using paper plates, another new technology at the time, and also used a combination of printing and photocopying in 1987 to publish 4 of my own books.

2 - Who or what was your main influence behind your decision to publish? These may include literary or non-literary influences.

As an artist I was interested in Beardsley's relationship with the likes of Oscar Wilde – that is as an artist working with the writer, the one in pictures the other with words. My first commissioned pieces of work were in black and white and they illustrated literary pieces in magazines like **Argot**, Victoria Universities literary magazine. They had very little relationship with Beardsley's works except that I too used pen and ink. I enjoyed Mark Williams' company and wit at the time and although some of his work was derivative it did have an energy that I liked. Particularly I liked its irreverence. Although I wrote some poetry in the late 60's and 70's there was nothing that was publishable although I was quite fond of it. The problem was that English was my second language and as a dyslexic I had problems with spelling and English as a subject at school but adored Greek poetry which I learned as a young boy in Cyprus. In the 60's I had a bit of a reputation as a graphic artist for **Argot, Cappicate, Salient,** all of which were University student publications. **Argot** was a literary magazine. There use to be a friendly rivalry between me who did drawings for **Cappicate** and Tom Scott and Bob Brockie who did art work for the Massey student magazine **Masquerade**. Through associating myself with people who write I suppose I thought that I'd be able to communicate some of my own thoughts . . . It wasn't until well after **Abecedary** that I thought that it would be good to publish some of my own drawings and it was only after that that I thought I may be able to attach to them some of the bits of writing I was scribbling out at the time. I suppose I thought photocopying allowed that to happen as it was a medium I discovered and then manipulated to get through good design results that looked as good as the real printed copy – well to the untrained eye. The type setting for **Abecedary** was done by

Olie Thomson a Danish type setter who emigrated from Denmark. He set himself up to Mt. Eden – Newton and was a master in his craft. From him I learned a lot about typography and page design. It wasn't until the late 70's that I started taking myself seriously as a poet and writer, although recently I remembered that at primary school in Cyprus our headmaster who used to collect our stories and keep them in a folder was adamant that I couldn't have them to bring to New Zealand with me when I asked for them. I sneaked into his office and stole them the day before our departure.At school in Cyprus we were brought up on stories and poetry by the best poets of the Greek culture. It wasn't until I was in London that I came across one of my favourite Greek poets Constantine Cavafy. I loved the novels of Kazantzakis from my teens when I came across a copy of **Zorba the Greek** in the Library at Wellington College.

The name One-Eyed Press came out of a conversation we were having with Ray Horsefull, a friend of Mark's who suggested a classical name in the tradition of Pegasus, Phoenix etc. and said "What about Cyclops?" I said a Kiwi would say something like "One-eyed" . . . and that's how One-Eyed Press came about.

3 - In your choice of authors was the main consideration for inclusion philosophical, literary or pragmatic?

The people that I published were initially friends, people who knew me and trusted me and who found it difficult to be published by the main literary presses.My criteria were always - work that I think is of merit and that had been rejected by other publishers. I decided that I would only publish poetry and because of that I knew that there was no money in it for me. Initially I subsidised my publications with putting in the work and the poets paying for the printing. Some I've even put money into them. I can't say either I or the poets that I published made money directly from their books, but the publishing did help though because it created a publishing record for them.I of course suffered from the "vanity press" label as I was forced to publish my own work. **The Muriwai Motel Sonnets** was favourably commented on by A.W. Reed Publishers in

Wellington when I was living in Auckland but as always they felt that I did not command a large enough audience to warrant their investment . . . so I had to publish it myself. I often wondered how many established N.Z. writers financed their first book but were able to keep it quiet as they achieved success and a higher profile.

4 - "...and if there is still a number of commissioned works which seem to have been dreamed up by a sabotaging office-boy on an LSD trip, there are now each year a growing quantity of books which worthily add to our literature." Professor J.C. Reid from an article introducing New Zealand Books in Print, written in 1968. I interpret Reid's assessment as an indication of the rift between the acceptable 'worthy' literature as endorsed by academia, and the new wave of sabotaging office boys and girls who at that time commissioned publishers to put out their works, or simply published things themselves, and in many cases the work of their friends. Comment on this quote in relation to the 'Vanity Press' vs 'Real Publishing' debate.

This is a vexed question ie. the one about Vanity Presses! Obviously there are publishers who for a price will publish peoples work whatever the standard and some of them make a decision to do just that. However in New Zealand unknown poets now who do not prescribe to university writer's classes have very few avenues for publication. There are in N.Z. several publishers who will charge you the cost of an edition and then quite happily claim your work as part of their own publishing list - implying that they paid the cost. Others though have certain fixed criteria for who they publish eg women's and Māori Writer presses, and in some instances they will strike a co-operative deal with the writer. I know of three New Zealand writers who paid to have their first books published. I am sure there are more. Many of the Vanity Presses are pretty up-front with what they offer. Many times writers actually paid printers to package and print their work and may have created an imprint to do it with. Photocopying freed publishing one's own work from the shackles of having to have lots of money in order to get the work out there. I have no problem with people publishing their own poetry. To me N.Z. will really be a mature society when a man or a woman sees as their coming of age in the production of their first book of poetry or short stories . . . a first step in achieving mana within our society.

5 - Initially, was your focus outwardly cosmopolitan or inwardly New Zealand looking, and how has this emphasis changed over the years?

I just wanted to get the books finished. I enjoyed the conceptual and development stages of the book despite finding it hard to work with printers - my focus was to freeze the words in time so that I could get them out of the way and move onto other writing. Publishing is a sort of completion of the poem - although there is the odd piece that I've gone back and changed. As at first I didn't see myself as a writer but an artist I tried to do things that did not necessarily fit in with good publishing practices. I wanted to make the books cheap and thus accessible but had to ensure that they were acceptable to people as books. So one was creating so-called collectable items but they were very transient because they were printed on cheap paper and the printing process did not lend itself to lasting a long time.I say this aware that 20 years or so after *The Muriwai Motel Sonnets* the copy that I have still looks alright. But at the time I didn't care about that. One of my in jokes was to have "limited editions" that had random numbers, sometimes 2 or 3 of the same number - it was my way of subverting the preciousness of what was the "Limited Edition" fad of the 70's and early 80's.I did over the years have a close friend who I worked with whom I met at my first exhibition at the Little Theatre at Auckland University and who went back to Australia. Michael Sharkey who now teaches at New England University (in N.S.W.) started Fat Possum Press . . . he and I decided to publish each others work and there's the odd book that refers to both imprints. Due to not being able to get the books sold because really there's no committed poetry market here in New

Zealand, we let this go. However, we are still great friends and he has been responsible for me presenting my work at poetry reading both in Armidale and Melbourne. What shocked me was how well a German audience received my work when I read it at the IXth Commonwealth Literature Conference in Laufen, West Germany in June 1986. The influences on my work have predominantly come from the Modern Greek poets. As New Zealand poetry was heavily influenced by U.S. post-modernism I was and still am seen as someone who one should not be bothered with despite winning poetry prizes. I think I've done a thorough apprenticeship in the craft experimenting with different forms from sonnet, haiku, ballad to blues etc. The diversity of style has been seen as a weakness despite several critics pointing that in the work there is a cohesive purpose. I think the best of my writing is encompassed in **The Desert** for which I have not as yet been able to get a publisher.

It should be noted that over the years as well as the books that I have published I have had seven exhibitions of drawings and paintings and one of photographs. That does not count group shows.

In the mid 1980's I applied for a grant to set up a truly multi-cultural magazine **Immigrant**. In this endeavour I was supported by poets like Riemke Ensing. The Arts Council turned me down.I wanted poets to be paid well for their work and I also wanted poetry to be promoted the same way that sport is promoted. My vision was, and I suppose it still is, that every New Zealander would have at least one poet's work that they went to find direction, solace, empathy or inspiration from.

6 - What were your methods of printing and distribution as a publisher? Did you receive any financial or other assistance from either public organisations, or private sponsorship?

For three books I had help from the Queen Elizabeth Arts Council. **After Looking For Broadway, Baron Lumbago** and **Mikrokosmos**. For my own work I received no financial help. The above three publications were printed by paper plates a cheap off-set process except the covers which were printed using metal plates. My 1987 books had the covers printed by plates but the content printed by photocopying. My first three books were a combination of photocopying the guts and printing the cover - although if I remember correctly **Abecedary** may have been printed on paper plates ie. offset.I remember been invited by Ron Holloway to visit him in South Auckland at his home. He tried to persuade me to get involved in hand press setting and printing but I recognised early that I did not have the patience for it. Working in the Rare Book Room had made me appreciate the craft of Printing but I was not convinced I should allow myself to be diverted from what I was trying to do . . . which was basically - to work to support my painting habit. Something that one could actually achieve in the seventies. NB Iain Sharp edited, typed and paid for the printing and other costs of his book - about $200

7 - How much of your publishing was commissioned and paid for (either fully or partially) by the author? Was your operation helped by the voluntary work of friends and family?

No publication was paid for fully by the author . . . I think. In all of them I put in the design, layout and distribution and most of the time they paid for the typesetting if it was required (I developed a technique which allowed typewritten text to be used saving about $600.00 on the cost - **Why Mammals Shiver** by Iain Sharp was done like that.)Many people helped me in one way or another. Writer David Ballantyne helped with ensuring that all books submitted to the Auckland Star were actually reviewed, even if it was a few lines by reviewers like David Hill. George Georgakakos a close friend helped me buy a computer in the mid-1980's on which I would type the work to overcome my dyslexia. Iain Sharp helped me with the collation of his book. Beryl Walker typed **Corrigendum** for me on a typewriter used by **Flash** (which became the **City Voice** - Newton, Grey Lynn, Westmere Community newspaper - I.B.M. machine with golf-ball type.) Most of the time I would mention those and other friends in the publications.NB Iain Sharp and John Bentley are to be given a lot of credit for their support of One-Eyed Press for which they proof-read the texts - and they did brilliant jobs on that.

8 - What has been the cost to you personally in terms of time, money and resources, of being involved in publishing in New Zealand? You may consider this in relation to more difficult areas such as relationships with friends, family etc. also.

It was always financially difficult. Whenever I had a job that paid reasonably well I would take on a publishing project. The only thing that stops me now is that teaching is an all-consuming affair. I never thought of this at the time but on hindsight financing those projects must have had some impact on my relationship with my partner . . . as I always seemed to be in debt.

9 - Where do you place yourself and your achievements as a publisher (and as a writer if applicable) in the history of the modern-day New Zealand literary scene? Do you feel that your contribution has been adequately acknowledged.

I think that One-Eyed Press has had considerable impact on the N.Z. literary scene. It published Mark Williams' and Iain Sharp's first books, it helped establish a cheaper form of publishing which has aided many Auckland writers getting published - see **Words on a Rotunda** - an Anthology of Auckland Poets edited by me but co-published by the Auckland City Council and One-Eyed Press. Also it published work by writers that other publishers had turned down eg. **Mikrokosmos, Baron Lumbago** and **After Looking for Broadway** . . . the latter an important contribution to N.Z. literature by Peter Olds. As well it has encouraged other writers who submitted manuscripts to go on and get their work published (eg. Rob Alan) and encouraged young writers (eg. John Pule). Because of

One Eyed Press I was involved in the poetry reading scene both here and Australia. I organised readings at the Rare Book Room in the Auckland Library where I worked pairing known and unknown poets together . . . and helped organise readings in many other venues in Dunedin (with Graham Lindsay, Kai Jensen and others) and Christchurch (with Michael Harlow and others). NB I'd like to see a system that exists in Cyprus where the poets publish their own books and then the State buys X number of copies from them that will cover their costs. The Cyprus Government then gives those books to visiting Heads of State or other visitors. If transposed to N.Z. this would introduce our literature to a wide variety of repositories around the world.

C.M. Kapiti, 2000.

Publisher: Original Books.

Niel Wright is a poet, novelist and critic. He has written from the grass-roots of New Zealand Aotearoa intellectual life for many years. His philosophy as a publisher is to get the text out into public institutions, rather than attempting to compete in the vagaries of the market place, therefore his print-runs are low, often no more than five or ten copies per book. This list is the bibliography of the work of Dr.F.W. Nielsen Wright as a publisher of the works of other writers. It does not include his own prolific output, the major item of which is his epic poem *The Alexandrians* which is on-going. Wright also publishes under the imprint Cultural and Political Booklets.

CRISP, Peter, **Shards**, 1998, Poetry

FORBES, Lindsay, **The Bearing Earth**, 1991, Poetry

GIBBS, Rowan, **Dorothy Quentin a la Recherche de la Madeleine Perdue**, 1998

GILBERT, Ruth, ***Early Poems 1938 - 1944***, 1988, Poetry

GILBERT, Ruth, ***More Early Poems 1939 - 1944***, 1988, Poetry

GILBERT, Ruth, ***Breathings***, 1992, Poetry

GILBERT, Ruth, ***Dream, Black Night's Child***, 1993, Poetry

GILBERT, Ruth, ***Complete Early Poems 1938 - 1944***, 1994, Poetry, also includes six later pieces

GILBERT, Ruth, ***Gongyla Remembers***, 1995, Poetry

HALES, J.S., ***Niel Wright and His Epic***, 1978, Criticism

HALES, J.S., ***Niel Wright and His Epic***, 1994, 2nd. Ed.

KELLY, John Liddell, ***Heine Poems***, 1985, Translation

KELLY, John Liddell, ***Heine and the Apocalypse***, 1997, Poetry and prose

LIST, Dennis, ***Falling off Chairs***, 1996, Poetry

LIST, Dennis, ***The Return of the Triboldies***, 1997, Novel

LLOYD, Trevor, ***A Walk Along Lambton Quay***, 1998, An exhibition of archae-art

LLOYD, Trevor, ***Stations Old Porirua Road***, 1998, An exhibition of archae-art

MACKAY, Jessie, ed., ***An Anthology of New Zealand Rhymes Old and New***, 1998, Poetry

MARSTON, John, ***The Metamorphosis of Pygmalion's Image***, 1989, Poetry

MORRALL, Barry, ***Poems for a TV Age***, 1989, Poetry

MORRALL, Barry, ***Wellington Hills, Wellington Skies***, 1989, Poetry

MORRALL, Barry, ***Alive and Screaming***, 1989, Poetry

MORRALL, Barry, ***Poems of Perth and Western Australia***, 1989, Poetry

MORRALL, Barry, ***Dangerously Close***, 1990, Poetry

O'CONNOR, Simon, ***An Irish Annal of Aotearoa (a Psycle-Drama)***, 1997, A play based on the novel ***The Irish Annals of New Zealand*** by Michael O'Leary

O'LEARY, Michael, ***Livin' ina Aucklan'***, 1998, Poetry, 2nd ed.

O'LEARY, Michael, ***Shake Speer's Faith***, 1998, Poetry

O'LEARY, Michael, ***Long, Dazed Journey into Night***, 1998, Part 2 of Work in Progress with drawings by the author

O'LEARY, Michael, ***Yellban Apocryphal***, 1999, Part 3 of Work in Progress

O'LEARY, Michael, ***Dream Reality***, 1999, Part 1 of Work in Progress

O'LEARY, Michael, ***It's All in the Mind You Know***, 1999, An essay on Samuel Beckett

O'LEARY, Michael, ***Float the Note***, 1999, Part 4 of Work in Progress, a novel ***Unlevel Crossings***

O'LEARY, Michael, ***Ka Atu I Kopua***, 1999, Poetry

O'LEARY, Michael, ***Straight***, 1999, Novel, 3rd ed. with drawings by Gregory O'Brien

O'LEARY, Michael, ***Out of It***, 1999, Novel, 2nd ed. with collages by Gregory O'Brien

O'LEARY, Michael, ***South: tu te makohu***, 1999, Part 5 of ***Unlevel Crossings***

O'LEARY, Michael, ***The Sow of Hades***, 1999, Part 6 of ***Unlevel Crossings,*** final installment plus an epilogue.

O'LEARY, Michael, ***Con Art: selected poems***, 1997, Poetry

O'LEARY, Michael, ***Noa / Nothing I: and other stories***, 1997, Short stories

O'LEARY, Michael, ***Aucklana Livinia Pluralla***, 1997, Prose, from Work in Progress

PARK, R.G., ***Parking Metres***, 1995, Poetry

PARK, R.G., ***Examples: A Thesaurus of Allusions Literary, Legendary and Historic***, 1997, Quotations

RICHMOND, Mary E., ***Poems 1914 - 1926***, 1997, Poetry

RICKETTS, Harry, ***Coming Under Scrutiny***, 1989, Rhymes

SANDERSON, Martyn, ***Michael O'Leary's Finger***, 1997, Screenplay, based on ***Straight,*** a novel by Michael O'leary

SHELLEY, Percy Bysshe, ***Prince Athanase and the Triumph of Life***, 1985, Poetic fragments integrated by Niel Wright

SHELLEY, Percy Bysshe, ***Adonaides***, 1989, Poetic fragments integrated by Niel Wright

SNADDEN, John Pine, ***Retrospect: Poems 1941 - 1994***, 1994, Poetry

SNADDEN, John Pine, ***From Under the Pile***, 1999, Poetry

TRAUE, J.E., ***Jet Log***, 1999, A bibliography

1 - What was your initial reason for getting involved in publishing? Please try to think of this in the spirit of what you were thinking and doing at the time.

I have had a sense of mission since I was 5, a sense of something to prove since I was 7 or 8. My earliest attempts to publish were made in 1947. My underlying motto is 'If I can I will'. In 1960 it was possible for me to publish and I began to do so through Pegasus Press. Once a publisher to that degree I was motivated to . . .

   (a) publish people and material that supported my own
       literary perspective,
   (b) to write material I saw as publishable.

The ability to publish then made it possible for me to pursue my literary interests, put another way, being able to publish empowered me as a writer and literary activist.

2 - Who or what was your main influence behind your decision to publish? These may include literary or non-literary influences.

See answer to 1.

3 - In your choice of authors was the main consideration for inclusion philosophical, literary or pragmatic?

See answer to 1.

4 - "...and if there is still a number of commissioned works which seem to have been dreamed up by a sabotaging office-boy on an LSD trip, there are now each year a growing quantity of books which worthily add to our literature." Professor J.C. Reid from an article introducing *New Zealand Books in Print*, written in 1968. I interpret Reid's assessment as an indication of the rift between the acceptable 'worthy' literature as endorsed by academia, and the new wave of sabotaging office boys and girls who at that time commissioned publishers to put out their works, or simply published things themselves, and in many cases the work of their friends. Comment on this quote in relation to the 'Vanity Press' vs 'Real Publishing' debate.

I have a great deal of respect for J.C. Reid as an anthologist and critic. One would have to go through the list of books he approved of to see how valid his judgement was. What he had in mind in contrast to what he approved of I do not understand from the quotation without more context.

How do you define Vanity Press?

My definition is that a Vanity Press produces output which is unsellable and in fact mainly never gets out of storage wherever. Any book or booklet that gets into circulation anywhich way is a legitimate publication. The only vanity publication is one that in fact goes nowhere.

My view is outside the long standing newspapers there has never been a publishing industry in Aotearoa. For the rest all book and booklet publications in Aotearoa have been due to small publishers, who are partly hobbyists, partly jobbing printers with a sideline;

invariably operations which were dependent on a leading individual or two and which did not outlast their careers.

In these terms the most successful of our small publishers have been those catering for the education market. This extends to something as big as the Reeds (AW,AH).

The university presses are little more than hobbyist publishers, such as for instance the Dunmore Press, our most productive publisher with 414 titles in the National Library on-line catalogue (where I have 386 under two imprints).

Overseas publishers have come into Aotearoa from time to time and done half a dozen or so titles over a five year period, then got out when they realize they couldn't cover their extravagant overheads (as opposed to the much smaller overheads of the local small publishers). The latest of these overseas publishers to come on shore is Random House (as Godwit). How long before they pull out?

Overwhelmingly small publishing in Aotearoa sees books sponsored or subsidised one way or another.

5 - Initially, was your focus outwardly cosmopolitan or inwardly New Zealand looking, and how has this emphasis changed over the years?

I am not interested in the world outside Aotearoa in terms of the choice of books I publish, but in fact I get overseas sales and am prepared to go after them. The market is the market and 'all orders will be filled' is my philosophy. There are now since 1995 more opportunities to tap the world market.

6 - What were your methods of printing and distribution as a publisher? Did you receive any financial or other assistance from either public organisations, or private sponsorship?

I do short print runs to order, so usually single photocopies.

I distribute by relying on the National Bibliography and other book data bases here and world wide to bring my publications to notice.

Once I got a $1500 grant from Lotto / Creative NZ, but capital is not a concern as I operate on a shoestring.

7 - How much of your publishing was commissioned and paid for (either fully or partially) by the author? Was your operation helped by the voluntary work of friends and family?

When I undertake to publish a book I do not ask the author to fork out, and I give six complimentary copies. But if the author wants more then I will do a deal for a quantity at an author's price (i.e. well below wholesale price).

I do all the work on my books as a hobby activity or buy in services (as an out of pocket expense).

8 - What has been the cost to you personally in terms of time, money and resources, of being involved in publishing in New Zealand? You may consider this in relation to more difficult areas such as relationships with friends, family etc. also.

Over the 40 years I have published I have carried a loss of about $500 a year at present day values. But my annual sales income has always covered 80% of my out of pocket expenses. So I see my publishing as a self-financing hobby in very large measure.

I have done as much publishing as I had time and resources to handle. In fact this averages about 10 books or booklets a year over 40 years, though most were published in the seven years I have been a full-time hobbyist, shall we say.

My literary interests in general have been very time consuming at the cost of relationships of course, not just private but also public.

I would calculate my outlay in time at 73,000 hours at $40 an hour, say $2,920,000 if anyone wants to pay me. The value of what

I have produced is incalculable, but I see it as setting up our National (Aotearoa) Literature as a multi-million dollar taonga.

9 - Where do you place yourself and your achievements as a publisher (and as a writer if applicable) in the history of the modern-day New Zealand literary scene? Do you feel that your contribution has been adequately acknowledged.

As a publisher I am the only one catering for the super intellectuals in Aotearoa as opposed to the mediocre types the rest address. I mean this quite frankly. As a writer I am the only writer in Aotearoa whose scale of work matches that of a major historic writer overseas.

As a poet I write and publish on average 600 lines a year.

As a prose writer I write the equivalent of 1500 printed pages a year, and publish about half that much a year.

I would need to have published 1000 books and booklets to get all my output into print. I have published over 450 to date.

As to recognition I have had this since I was 14 years old (when my short stories won prizes). There isn't any criteria by which to judge my performance as a publisher and writer that doesn't give me status that gratifies. I am not aware what more would be required in any real practical way. I would welcome more sales, but that would involve more hard work and therefore more than a one man business.

The books of authors I publish as ORIGINAL BOOKS usually reach print runs between 25 and 65 copies. One went over 400.

F.W.N.W. Wellington, 2000.

Publisher: Pemmican Press.

Chris Orsman is a poet and publisher noted for his production of finely crafted works, both in the words and their presentation on the printed page.

AITCHISON, Johanna, ***Oh My God I'm Flying***, 1999, Poetry

DAVIDSON, Lynn, ***Mary Shelley's Window***, 1999, Poetry

HORROCKS, Ingrid, ***Natsukashii***, 1998, Poetry

MacPHERSON, Mary, ***The Inland Eye***, 1998, Poetry

MANHIRE, Bill et al., ***"Homelight": an Antarctic Miscellany***, 1998, Words and images, with Nigel Brown and Chris Orsman

MANHIRE, Bill et al., ***Southern Convergence***, 1999, Antarctic art, with Chris Orsman, Margaret Mahy, Nigel Brown and Margaret Eliot.

ORSMAN, Chris, ***Black South***, 1997, Poetry

ORSMAN, Chris, ed., ***Pemmican: an Annual Magazine of Poetry***, 1998, Poetry

O'SULLIVAN, Vincent, ***I'll Tell You This Much***, 2000, Poetry

PLUMB, Vivienne, ***Avalanche***, 2000, Poetry

RICKETTS, Harry, ***13 Ways***, 1997, Poetry

SEWELL, Bill, ***El Sur***, 1998, Poetry

*The average print run for Pemmican Press is 100 copies.

1 - What was your initial reason for getting involved in publishing? Please try to think of this in the spirit of what you were thinking and doing at the time.

Initially, I was interested in self-publishing my collection **Black South.** Talking with Harry Ricketts one day, he mentioned that he had a small collection of poetry ready, and we decided to publish that, too. The Press grew from there. It struck both Harry and I that there was room for small hand-bound fine editions of poetry - something between mainstream publications (VUP, AUP etc.) and self-publication. Also, it was our conviction that poetry, as a fairly under-valued art in New Zealand, deserves care and consideration in its publication, especially in terms of layout and typography. In other words, by producing quality editions at affordable prices we are signalling something of the general value of poetry.

2 - Who or what was your main influence behind your decision to publish? These may include literary or non-literary influences.

My personal model for fine verse editions was the work of the Wai-te-ata Press in Wellington, under the direction of Professor Don McKenzie. In particular, I remember fine editions of Alistair Camp-bell (**Blue Rain, Sanctuary of Spirits**) and Bill Manhire's classic collection **How to Take Your Clothes Off at the Picnic.**

3 - In your choice of authors was the main consideration for inclusion philosophical, literary or pragmatic?

Literary and pragmatic. We have tended to publish local (i.e. Wellington) authors because these are the ones we meet and hear about. Recommendations from interested parties has been the main way we hear of collections. We have had quite a lot of mss submitted to us, but I don't think we've yet published an unsolicited ms.

4 - "...and if there is still a number of commissioned works which seem to have been dreamed up by a sabotaging office-boy on an LSD trip, there are now each year a growing quantity of books which worthily add to our literature." Professor J.C. Reid from an article introducing *New Zealand Books in Print*, written in 1968. I interpret Reid's assessment as an indication of the rift between the acceptable 'worthy' literature as endorsed by academia, and the new wave of sabotaging office boys and girls who at that time commissioned publishers to put out their works, or simply published things themselves, and in many cases the work of their friends. Comment on this quote in relation to the 'Vanity Press' vs 'Real Publishing' debate.

I can't say that I've been aware of such a debate. Pemmican Press is careful to preserve the apparatus of real publishing in regard to bearing all the costs of publication and paying decent royalties on copies sold. The range of new (or newish) small presses bears testimony to the vigour of the poetry scene in New Zealand.

5 - Initially, was your focus outwardly cosmopolitan or inwardly New Zealand looking, and how has this emphasis changed over the years?

Our focus has always been to publish distinctive small collections of verse by both new and established New Zealand writers. This emphasis has remained unchanged. The content of collections varies, from the locally specific, to more universal themes, but there is no editorial prescription for what a collection may contain.

6 - What were your methods of printing and distribution as a publisher? Did you receive any financial or other assistance from either public organisations, or private sponsorship?

Printing is done on laser and inkjet printers attached to a PC. All binding and cutting is done by hand. Pemmican does its own distribution, and we receive no financial assistance from other organisations.

7 - How much of your publishing was commissioned and paid for (either fully or partially) by the author? Was your operation helped by the voluntary work of friends and family?

None of our publications was commissioned or paid for by an author. Our operation involved no voluntary work.

8 - What has been the cost to you personally in terms of time, money and resources, of being involved in publishing in New Zealand? You may consider this in relation to more difficult areas such as relationships with friends, family etc. also.

Pemmican Press is self-supporting but does not make a profit as such as neither Harry Ricketts nor Chris Orsman receive payment for their work. The main outlay is in terms of time, which is considerable. This involvement does mean less time for other interests, e.g.. one's own writing.

9 - Where do you place yourself and your achievements as a publisher (and as a writer if applicable) in the history of the modern-day New Zealand literary scene? Do you feel that your contribution has been adequately acknowledged.

Yes, Pemmican has gained a small reputation for producing quality books of verse and giving new writers a first publication. It has a modest place in the literary and publishing history of the late 'nineties and early twenty-first century. This place has been acknowledged - in reviews, etc.

C.O. Wellington, 2000.

Publisher: Prometheus Press.

Donald Kerr is a poet and editor of *Echoes, Good Wine and Glass: poetry, prose, art 1,2,3 and 4*. Kerr now works as the Rare Books librarian at the Auckland Public Library.

ENSING, Riemke, **Topographies**, 1984, Poetry, with graphics by Nigel Brown

POTOCKI de MONTALK, Count Geoffrey, **Recollections of My Fellow Poets**, 1983, Memoir

Journals

KERR, Donald, ed., **Echoes, Good Wine and Glass: poetry, prose, art**, 1983, Literary Magazine

KERR, Donald, ed., **Echoes 2: (poetry, prose, art)**, 1983, Literary Magazine

KERR, Donald, ed., **Echoes 3: (poetry, prose, art)**, 1984, Literary Magazine

KERR, Donald, ed., **Echoes 4: (poetry, prose, art)**, 1984, Literary Magazine

1 - What was your initial reason for getting involved in publishing? Please try to think of this in the spirit of what you were thinking and doing at the time.

To provide an alternative outlet for up and coming, and established writers and poets. At the time - the early 80's - there seemed to be so few around.

2 - Who or what was your main influence behind your decision to publish? These may include literary or non-literary influences.

Irving Steltner's **Stroker** magazine; a New York based publication offering prose, poetry and art. It was an excellent model and relatively cheap to produce.

3 - In your choice of authors was the main consideration for inclusion philosophical, literary or pragmatic?

I tried to remain objective when choosing materials. The driving force was to offer variety and something different, a little out of the ordinary in NZ.

A certain amount of pragmatism was evident: could only choose from what I received.

4 - "...and if there is still a number of commissioned works which seem to have been dreamed up by a sabotaging office-boy on an LSD trip, there are now each year a growing quantity of books which worthily add to our literature." Professor J.C. Reid from an article introducing *New Zealand Books in Print*, written in 1968. I interpret Reid's assessment as an indication of the rift between the acceptable 'worthy' literature as endorsed by academia, and the new wave of sabotaging office boys and girls who at that time commissioned publishers to put out their works, or simply published things themselves, and in many cases the work of their friends. Comment on this quote in relation to the 'Vanity Press' vs 'Real Publishing' debate.

Vanity printing has a long and honourable history and it is a valid exercise considering the diminished risk taking by established publishing firms.

Admittedly some vanity printing publications should not see the light of day, but they do add up to a significant body of work and reflect something of the times, movements etc.

5 - Initially, was your focus outwardly cosmopolitan or inwardly New Zealand looking, and how has this emphasis changed over the years?

Most definitely outwardly cosmopolitan: cannot comment on the changes.

6 - What were your methods of printing and distribution as a publisher? Did you receive any financial or other assistance from either public organisations, or private sponsorship?

Method of printing: jobbed out to a commercial firm (Osborne Printing).

Distribution: I was working as a publisher's rep and this involved yearly trips to the university towns in NZ. I was able to contact booksellers/others direct. This sort of moonlighting was essential for sales.

Assistance: At the time **Echoes** was published the policy was to be a proven stayer before any money was shelled out. You had to have a proven track record which of course meant that once you had done 3 or 4 one is broke! Poets are notorious at not paying for books they are in.

The proven track record policy changed later and became a "merit" one: For Ensing's **Topographies** I received $600 from the Arts Council.

Countrywide sponsored a short story competition to the tune of $200 only - winner published in Echoes 4.

Overall no assistance; result large bill with a friendly printer. The latter a most necessary thing.

7 - How much of your publishing was commissioned and paid for (either fully or partially) by the author? Was your operation helped by the voluntary work of friends and family?

No payment at all to poets/writers. They did receive one free copy of **Echoes**. In the case of Riemke's work I gave her copies (20 ?) for personal distribution. Potocki's - can't honestly remember.

Operation: Selection of pieces for Echoes - especially 2,3 and 4 were done by friends; Iain Sharp, Elizabeth Newton, John Gascots, O'Leary etc. Very casual.

8 - What has been the cost to you personally in terms of time, money and resources, of being involved in publishing in New Zealand? You may consider this in relation to more difficult areas such as relationships with friends, family etc. also.

Large bills at the printers which eventually got paid. As previously mentioned, I was lucky to have such an understanding printer. Publication of such works do take time and effort and at times it is seen as a thankless task; under-appreciated, sales figures low (non-existent). Overall a worthwhile experience which I am glad I did.

Anyone embarking on such a venture needs to consider marketing and promotion. Ongoing, ongoing, ongoing!!!

9 - Where do you place yourself and your achievements as a publisher (and as a writer if applicable) in the history of the modern-day New Zealand literary scene? Do you feel that your contribution has been adequately acknowledged.

a footnote in history !

a footnote in NZ Private press periodical/history.
a footnote.

D.K. Auckland, 2000.

Publisher: Puriri Press.

John Denny is seen in the small publishing fraternity as a fine printer and craftsman, an exponent of the book as a finished artwork, an aesthetic entity. As well as his own two imprints, Pettifogging and Puriri Presses, Denny has printed work of significance for other publishers including Brick Row, The Griffin Press, Slightly Foxed, the Dragonfly Press, Waiata Koa and Illyria Press.

As Pettifogging Press

ALLSOP, Joyce, ***The Voyage of the Gale***, 1982, Autobiography (100 copies)

BELL, Angela, ***Roses and Lilacs***, 1983, Fiction, poetry etc. (150 copies)

BISHOP, Nicholas, ***The Feijoa Patch***, 1985, Fiction, autobiography (60 copies)

BLACKWELL, Simon, ***Warnings***, 1982, Poetry (100 copies)

BRANDON, Gillian, ***Mangamingi Poems***, 1980, Poetry (100 copies)

DENNY, Alexander William, ***The Years Between***, 1985, Autobiography (150 copies)

DENNY, Heather, ed., ***The Best of Password - (I, II, III, IV, V) with Puriri Press***, 1981 to 1998, Education (between 100 and 600 copies)

DENNY, John, ***Magic Squares and Pendulums***, 1987, Mathematics (50 copies)

DENNY, John, ***Specimens***, 1984, Type specimens (75 copies)

DENNY, John, ***Wharfdale: The Story of a Printing Press***, 1987, History (150 copies)

ELMER, Ron, ***Footeye***, 1984, Fiction (60 copies)

MANN, Barbara, ***The Russian Doll***, 1981, Poetry (100 copies)

PARKINSON, Phil, ***An Ode for Turnbull Library***, 1981, Poetry (60 copies)

PARKINSON, Phil, ***Halymenia***, 1980, Scientific (100 copies)

PARKINSON, Phil, ***Iridea***, 1981, Scientific (100 copies)

PARKINSON, Phil, ***Grateloupia***, 1980, Scientific (100 copies)

STOKES, Ida, ***Let Me Serve You a Poem***, 1983, Poetry (150 copies)

STOVER, Enid, ***Echoes*** , 1984, Poetry (110 copies)

SWAINSON, William, ***A Review of the Art of Colonisation***, 1987, Historical (220 copies)

WILLIACY, Martella, ***A Rose of Hard Coral***, 1983, Poetry (300 copies)

As Puriri Press

BETH'EL, Aaron, **Sacred Promise**, 1993, Poetry (308 copies)

BETH'EL, Aaron, **The Book of Love**, 1991, Poetry (350 copies)

BURLEIGH, Lois, **Inside Outside**, 1991, Letters (200 copies)

DENNY, Alexander , **Barefoot Days and other Stories**, 1990, Autobiography (200 copies)

DENNY, John, **A Decade With a Dinosaur**, 1989, History (250 copies)

FOX, Nancy, **Landmarks**, 1989, Poetry (200 +200 copies)

GAUDIN, Marie, **Brief Singing**, 1988, Poetry (100 copies)

GREGORY, Brian, **Katherine Mansfield, our missing contemporary**, 1991, Quotations (60 copies)

GREGORY, Brian, **Portraits of the Artist**, 1991, Poetry (100 copies)

JOHNSON, Arthur, **Lettering on Books**, 1993, Educational (250 copies)

LA HATTE, Nadine, **New Myths for Old Landscapes**, 1990, Poetry (120 copies)

LA HATTE, Nadine, **Celebrating Stones**, 1995, Poetry (150 copies)

LAND, Peter, **My Tao**, 1990 , Translations (300 copies)

LONEY, Alan, **Envoy** , 1996, Poetry (200 copies)

MANN, Barbara, ***Your Snow Falls in Summer***, 1989, Poetry (200 copies)

O'BRIEN, Gregory, ***The Long Fall From Splendour to Splendour***, 1993, Poetry (95 copies)

RIDDELL, Ron, ***Michaelangelo Dreams***, 1997, Poetry (200 copies)

RIDDELL, Ron, ***Love Songs for the Dead***, 1999, Poetry (50 copies)

ROSS, Emily, ***Oranges and Lemons***, 1994, Poetry (120 copies)

SCHOLTEN, Carolyn, ***Lost at the South Pole***, 1997, Nature (40 copies)

SHAW, Helen, ***I Listen***, 1995, Meditations (200 copies)

1 - What was your initial reason for getting involved in publishing? Please try to think of this in the spirit of what you were thinking and doing at the time.

I began in 1975 as a hobby printer with a little Adana press and half a dozen cases of type. At first I printed quaint cards for my own amusement. Later I was given an Arab treadle platen, which hooked me on real printing and enabled me to print a much larger page area and quantity of material.

In early 1979 I bought a Linotype machine from the Auckland Star, and a friend of mine, Phil Parkinson of Wellington, persuaded me that I now had the wherewithal to print books - he had a series of publications in mind, and I undertook to produce these for the cost of materials, in order to learn the skills needed for operating the Linotype and for printing an entire book - and for the hell of it; it was becoming an absorbing hobby. The name I adopted, Pettifogging Press, reflected my amusement at the seriousness with which some other small presses took their work.

I became Puriri Press for most purposes when I became a small business at the beginning of 1988; several people had expressed discomfort at being associated with the hobby name and it is now used only rarely.

But I must emphasise that it was the process of designing, printing and binding - making books, that was my primary desire, and this has remained my strongest motivation, not publishing as such.

2 - Who or what was your main influence behind your decision to publish? These may include literary or non-literary influences.

Phil Parkinson was extremely influential at this time, in that he provided much worthwhile material, which is a huge difficulty for the newly established printer - what do you print? Here was a series of real, live, unpublished scientific texts of undoubted merit which had been ignored by the scientific community because it didn't fit in with the theories of those currently 'in charge' of what got published in journals. This appealed to me far more than simply reproducing yet another edition of William Blake or whatever.

My wife's sister had an appealing set of poems which became my second book.

Phil Parkinson later provide the text for Swainson's Review of **The Art of Colonisation**, a valuable reprint of a rare historical publication.

As stated previously, the other strong factor was my own fascination with books and how they are made, in every sense, which I have had since childhood.

3 - In your choice of authors was the main consideration for inclusion philosophical, literary or pragmatic?

The latter initially, it was whatever came along, because I liked producing books. As time went by I got more discriminating, as the commitment had to be worth it - I had to like the content of what I was printing as well as enjoying the process. But finding suitable material remains tricky; I am publishing less myself these days, and lack of interesting texts is an important reason, though not the only one.

4 - "...and if there is still a number of commissioned works which seem to have been dreamed up by a sabotaging office-boy on an LSD trip, there are now each year a growing quantity of books which worthily add to our literature." Professor J.C. Reid from an article introducing *New Zealand Books in Print*, written in 1968. I interpret Reid's assessment as an indication of the rift between the acceptable 'worthy' literature as endorsed by academia, and the new wave of sabotaging office boys and girls who at that time commissioned publishers to put out their works, or simply published things themselves, and in many cases the work of their friends. Comment on this quote in relation to the 'Vanity Press' vs 'Real Publishing' debate.

I have always reserved the term 'vanity press' for those publishers who really entice people to provide material for them to have printed, basically for the benefit of the publisher. The pattern is to charge a large amount of money and do very little in terms of advertising or distribution. The vanity publisher is seldom a printer, but a middleman maximising profit for himself.

There is a clear distinction in my mind between vanity publishing and self-publishing. It is obvious that the established publishers will naturally never, or seldom, print anything they can't make a profit on, and that the university presses only do it because their books are largely funded by the taxpayer, both through grants and reduced production costs. But lots of texts are continually being written which merit publication yet will never succeed in the larger marketplace. By all means put it out yourself - some very well known NZ writers have started this way - but you don't go to a vanity publisher and spend a fortune.

My production philosophy has been quite simply that my 'thing' is producing fine books to the best of my ability, and if someone wants a book produced I could be keen on doing it. I have to earn something for my work, but try to keep costs to a minimum and if the author wants to be involved I can assist them to do as much of the work as their skill / time allows. I will advise from my experience on the edition size, etc.

However, because I would rather be printing the next book than selling the previous one, marketing is largely the concern of the author. If I'm really keen on a book I'll publish it myself, though even then the author would need to be prepared to assist on the marketing side, my weak point.

I do not deceive people; nor do I advertise for work, people seek me out. The books I have produced over the years all have a certain charm, some are really special, and some are quite important in a small way, though no doubt their literary merit varies greatly.

5 - Initially, was your focus outwardly cosmopolitan or inwardly New Zealand looking, and how has this emphasis changed over the years?

Pettifogging / Puriri Press just naturally began producing New Zealand material, because most of the authors were people living locally; the subject matter was mostly poetry or non-fiction - hence it dealt with mainly New Zealand issues / history.

No real policy, it's just the way things were / are; but I wouldn't call it inward looking!

6 - What were your methods of printing and distribution as a publisher? Did you receive any financial or other assistance from either public organisations, or private sponsorship?

I did all my own designing, printing (letterpress, from metal type) and binding until 1992, when the addition of computer technology allowed me to typeset books with huge amounts of text that could not be set in metal and printed by one person. At this point I began getting some books printed on the Docu Tech (high-speed photocopying), but I always did the typesetting and finishing myself. Just this year, 2000, I am able to take back all the work myself as a result of the purchase of a high-capacity laser printer. My mix now is about one third metal, two thirds electronic.

Puriri Press has never received any grants or sponsorship. Occasionally others in the production process have: e.g.. in the case of *I Listen*, Debbie Grossman Knowles had received a grant for editing the material, but that was before I became involved. In fact this production was funded entirely by Puriri Press.

Another case was Beth Sergeant for *The Visionary*, for which she had QEII assistance - but this was arranged by her, I guess I received some of this indirectly in payment for my share of the work; Beth published the book herself.

I did consider asking for support once or twice, but was always put off by the requirements for a minimum of 500 copies, a number which few of my publications reached. I later learned that many people broke this rule, and apparently it didn't really matter.

Of course later work for other publishers such as Brick Row had regular QEII / Creative NZ funding, but again, I had nothing to do with that process - I was simply the printer, and was paid for what I did, and these books are not produced under my imprint.

7 - How much of your publishing was commissioned and paid for (either fully or partially) by the author? Was your operation helped by the voluntary work of friends and family?

At first when I was a hobby press, it was the normal pattern for the author to pay, though they only paid actual production costs and I worked for nothing.

Later there was a mix of the two - at first I didn't really know what a publisher's role was. When I became a small business I became less keen on having authors pay for books under my imprint - gradually I assumed the financial burden myself when publishing under Puriri Press. In cases of self-publishing, many of the authors chose their imprint and the book went out under that name. Some were already established publishers, such as the Griffin Press.

In many cases authors, friends and family collated, folded and sewed, though I always did the more complex parts of the process myself.

8 - What has been the cost to you personally in terms of time, money and resources, of being involved in publishing in New Zealand? You may consider this in relation to more difficult areas such as relationships with friends, family etc. also.

This has never been seen by me or my family as negative in any respect. It is true that I gave up a teaching salary in 1988 in order to become Puriri Press, but that was a lifestyle choice which I have never regretted. We have earned much less money as a household, but I have spent my time doing what I wanted to do, and that is beyond price. My family has always been fully supportive, as they share this philosophy; so I am very fortunate; I have known other people lose everything because of their devotion to small publishing.

9 - Where do you place yourself and your achievements as a publisher (and as a writer if applicable) in the history of the modern-day New Zealand literary scene? Do you feel that your contribution has been adequately acknowledged.

It's probably too early to assess the real merit of a small press such as mine - posterity will decide.

Being a self-contained and self-motivated person, I have pretty well ignored the response or otherwise to my work. I know that people recommend me and seek me out to handle their books, and that is recognition enough most of the time.

I guess mine is a reasonably good contribution to the small press scene, but I am not really able to judge on the basis of literary significance. Slight, I would say, as none of the authors I have dealt with have become well known, but some of the books will certainly have a long term value in recording aspects of life and thought in this country.

J.D. Auckland, 2000.

Publisher: Spiral Collective.

Heather McPherson is a respected poet and writer in this country, she is well-known as one of the leading lights in the feminist movement and a strong advocate for equal rights for the gay and lesbian community.

BACHMANN, Marina, ***Drawing Together***, 1985, Poetry, with Janet Charman and Sue Fitchett

BAXTER, Hilary, ***The Other Side of Dawn***, 1987, Poetry

CHERRY, Frances, ***Washing Up in Parrot Bay***, 1999, Novel, published in association with Steele Roberts

EVANS, Marian, ed., ***A Womens Picture Book: Twenty Five Women Artists from Aotearoa New Zealand***, 1986, Art, with Tilly Lloyd and Bridie Lonie

FITCHETT, Sue , ***Charts and Soundings: Some Small Navigation Aids***, 1999, Navigation, with Jane Zusters

HULME, Keri, ***the bone people***, 1983, Novel

McPHERSON, Heather, *A Figurehead: a Face*, 1982, Poetry, cover illustrator; Anna Keir

McPHERSON, Heather, et al., *Spiral 7*, 1992, A collection of lesbian art and writing from Aotearoa New Zealand, with Marian Evans, Pamela Gerrish Nunn, and Julie King, eds.

SAJ, *Amazon Songs*, 1987, Poetry

STURM, J.C., *The House of the Talking Cat*, 1983, Stories

Wahine Kaituhi: Women Writers of Aotearoa, 1985, An anthology of New Zealand women writers

as Old Bags Press

McPHERSON, Heather, *Other World Relations*, 1990, Poetry

Journal

Spiral: Womens' Art Magazine, 1976 to 1993, Poems, prose, artwork, photography etc.

1 - What was your initial reason for getting involved in publishing? Please try to think of this in the spirit of what you were thinking and doing at the time.

The context was the early seventies. I'd had poems published in *Landfall* and approached Leo Bensemann, then Caxton Press and *Landfall* editor, with a collection. I mentioned that I had become a feminist. He said that Rita Cook - Rita Angus - had become a feminist "but it didn't do her any good either." He said that yes, my poems were publishable but to go away and get a grant.

I didn't know how to do this. The book languished unpublished. Some time (and a child) later, in a group called S.H.E. (Sisters for Homophile Equality) I was working on a Homosexual Law Reform submission. It was a large group, my input was negligible. But the experience spurred me into thinking what I would prefer to be doing. With the general excitement of Women's and Gay Liberation in the air, with a number of talented women artists in the group, with their stories of being turned down for publication or by art galleries, I thought I would rather be working with/for women artists.

I made contact with Don Long and Alan Loney who had contacts with American small press associations. Both were helpful and supportive and I printed off flyers on one of their elderly printing presses for a women artists group. The physical work was tiring; I realised that the priority for me was not beautiful and/or old-style printing but getting the work out.

A little before that time Robin Sivewright and Jill Hannah had set up Herstory Press in Wellington and were printing off Womens' Liberation material & posters & pamphlets. We negotiated; Katherine Algie, Allie Eagle, Patsy Keene, Zusters, Morrigan, Saj, Paulette Barr and other women, we put together a first issue and Herstory printed it.

2 - Who or what was your main influence behind your decision to publish? These may include literary or non-literary influences.

Womens Liberation - and the stories of women artists (in the widest sense of painters, writers, photographers, sculptors etc.) of being turned down by publishers and galleries.

A spirit of defiance strode abroad . . . Some of our ideas were . . . Art is not made in a vacuum but out of our lives. Women's and men's lives are different experiences of socialization, child-rearing. Thus women and men artists have and express different values as well as content. Sexism both causes and affects women's marginalisation in the arts by overt and covert censorship of women's experiences as acceptable art content.

In the same way, homophobia censors the expression of lesbian and gay experiences in the arts. Women artists - some great - have been overlooked and dismissed by male gatekeepers of the literary and artistic canon. Publishing and art selection in New Zealand as elsewhere being male-dominated gave little support to women writers and artists and often actively discouraged us.

I was familiar with the story of Walt Whitman's self-publication, also of various founders U.S. small magazines such as Margaret Anderson's **Little Review.** (My primary school experience of making a magazine had some influence also?) The most profound influence on my thinking initially was **The First Sex** By Elizabeth Gould Davis and a little later, **How to Suppress Women's Writing** by Joanna Russ.

3 - In your choice of authors was the main consideration for inclusion philosophical, literary or pragmatic?

All three considerations operated. We advertised for women only and printed only what we received. We had a feminist agenda.

But there is a process in defining what is meant by 'feminist' & what is meant by 'feminist artist' - and our ideas changed over time. For instance, the sixties for women artists had been notorious for the "suicide syndrome" - the brilliant women artists as depressive and/or self-destructive (e.g. Plath, Arbus). As feminists in the early seventies our context was that we wanted positive portraits of strong women, we wanted celebrations of being women/lesbian etc., we wanted to erase the images of sex symbol or victim. I once turned down some good work because it was too 'depressing'; if I now question that decision I also note that the writer became very successful in the mainstream. Similar political/philosophical issues arose later with the Womens Gallery e.g.. over women artists showing images of men.

4 - "...and if there is still a number of commissioned works which seem to have been dreamed up by a sabotaging office-boy on an LSD trip, there are now each year a growing quantity of books which worthily add to our literature." Professor J.C. Reid from an article intro-

ducing *New Zealand Books in Print,* written in 1968. I interpret Reid's assessment as an indication of the rift between the acceptable 'worthy' literature as endorsed by academia, and the new wave of sabotaging office boys and girls who at that time commissioned publishers to put out their works, or simply published things themselves, and in many cases the work of their friends. Comment on this quote in relation to the 'Vanity Press' vs 'Real Publishing' debate.

Since the reasons for our Spiral publishing venture were political - sexism, racism and homophobia are political/gatekeeping issues by which a mainstream majority culture suppresses, censors or disregards minority concerns - I have nothing to say on the above issue.

Except that long may political publishing flourish, and if political publishing - to extend limits/boundaries, to give a political minority a voice - is considered a Vanity Press concept, long may Vanity Presses prosper and flourish.

5 - Initially, was your focus outwardly cosmopolitan or inwardly New Zealand looking, and how has this emphasis changed over the years?

Initially, much feminist and Women Artists Movement theory came from overseas, particularly the United Kingdom and the United States. With growing confidence, we women/artists applied & modified it to New Zealand conditions in our own consciousness-raising groups.

Our main focus was to publish New Zealand women, to build connections and rapprochements between artists working in different media and to get New Zealand women's' art and voices heard overseas; there was in the seventies quite a vital exchange of arts magazines with Australia, the UK and the US feminist presses.

I have not been involved in Spiral publishing since *Spiral 7* and am not aware of changes in policy.

6 - What were your methods of printing and distribution as a publisher? Did you receive any financial or other assistance from either public organisations, or private sponsorship?

Printing of first issues was done by the feminist Herstory Press. Later local printing presses were used - the magazine was typeset, laid-out and mocked up to printing quality.

Distribution was always a problem. The women's' community in Christchurch (where the first 4 issues originated) helped; the Women's bookstores and Broadsheet (in Auckland), were helpful; individual members of each collective did much wonderful work to get *Spiral* throughout the country. The first four *Spiral* issues were, apart from sales, subscriptions and donations, mostly funded by the Christchurch women's/lesbian community dances. When a sales cash box disappeared at a conference, the Spiral collective held a special dance to replace the stolen money. Briefly, the distributing was voluntary, both it and fund-raising communal.

7 - How much of your publishing was commissioned and paid for (either fully or partially) by the author? Was your operation helped by the voluntary work of friends and family?

Spiral could not have existed without the wonderful voluntary support of friends, partner(s) and the Christchurch lesbian community. The first issue's loose pages were laid out in Saj's living room of The Blue House and literally stapled together by about a dozen women - the house's occupants and the Spiral collective.

I guess the authors paid their time, paper, postage. For the first issue(s?) we gave the authors a magazine and a token payment ($2)(!) to acknowledge their 'work'; this was to be augmented but we never made enough money to fully cover expenses. I don't remember when we stopped the token payment; nor what happened after I left the collective (after issue 4, returning to share the editorial role for issue 7).

8 - What has been the cost to you personally in terms of time, money and resources, of being involved in publishing in New Zealand? You may consider this in relation to more difficult areas such as relationships with friends, family etc. also.

The cost . . . mmmm, I have tended to think rather of rewards - to have been in an exciting venture in an exciting time, to have met many talented artists, to have made life-long friendships and argued and worked with some wonderful women, good at their jobs - writers, artists, printers, layout artists or whatever . . . also to see the inspiration continue, so that later women's' collectives published under the name/imprint (e.g. ***the bone people***) . . . I guess one cost was extra stress - a solo mother raising a son and doing a part-time paid job to augment my benefit, I never had any spare cash let alone being able to subsidize a magazine. The other cost was having little time for my own writing - I relinquished my involvement with the collective to write more.

9 - Where do you place yourself and your achievements as a publisher (and as a writer if applicable) in the history of the modern-day New Zealand literary scene? Do you feel that your contribution has been adequately acknowledged.

I place myself in an accident of herstory - being the person in the place at the time when a conjunction of interests - personal and political - offered the opportunity, with other women, to make a statement about women's work . . .

Re the second question - do I feel my contribution has been adequately acknowledged - I'd have to ask **by whom?** By the New Zealand literary scene? It could be surprising to be acknowledged at all, given some of the hostile editorializing at the time . . . and I'd rather be acknowledged for my writing. But by women artists and friends? Yes. By feminist herstorians? Yes.

(I place myself in an accident of herstory - being the person in the place at the time when a conjunction of interests - personal and political - offered the opportunity, with other women, to make a statement about women's work . . .

Re the second question - do I feel my contribution has been adequately acknowledged - I'd have to ask **by whom?** By the New Zealand literary scene? It could be surprising to be acknowledged at all, given some of the hostile editorializing at the time . . . and I'd rather be acknowledged for my writing. But by women artists and friends? Yes. By feminist herstorians? Yes.)

H.McP. Hamilton, 2000.

Publisher: Steele Roberts.

Roger Steele is dedicated to having a book of New Zealand poetry beside every bed. His attempt to fulfill this vision has lead to the production of some of the finest volumes, both in content and presentation, in New Zealand in recent years.

CHERRY, Frances, **Washing Up in Parrot Bay**, 1999, Novel, with Spiral Collective (1500 copies)

COLQUHOUN, Glenn, **The Art of Walking Upright**, 1999, Poetry (1000 copies)

FAWKES, Glenda, **A Talent for Flight**, 1999, Poetry, with images by Claire Beynon (500 copies)

GINN, Noel, **Dweller on the Threshold**, 1998, Memoir, edited by Paul Millar (500 copies)

HAGER, Mandy, **Run for the Trees**, 1999, Poetry (2000 copies)

LEIBRICH, Julie, **Paper Road**, 1998, Poetry (500 copies)

MIDDLETON, O.E., ***The Big Room & Other Stories***, 1999, Stories (500 copies)

NEUTZE, Guyon, ***Dark Out of Darkness***, 1999, Poetry, with images by Jurgen Waibel (250 copies)

O'SULLIVAN, Brendan, ***Wetamorphosis***, 1998, Satire, with Bo Stent

POTIKI, Roma, ***Shaking the Tree***, 1998, Poetry, with illustrations by Dorothy Waetford (800 copies)

POWELL, Anne, ***Firesong***, 1999, Poetry (1600 copies)

RICHARDSON, Paddy, ***The Company of a Daughter***, 2000, Fiction (1500 copies)

STURM, J.C., ***Dedications***, 1996, Poetry, with illustrations by John Baxter (1000 copies)

TUWHARE, Hone, ***Shape-shifter***, 1997, Poetry, illustrated by Shirley Grace (2000 copies)

URALE, Makerita, ***The Magic Seashell***, 1998, Playscript, with illustrations by Samuel Sakaria (3000 copies)

WEATHERHEAD, Diane, ***The Pink Filing Cabinet***, 1998, Fiction

1 - What was your initial reason for getting involved in publishing? Please try to think of this in the spirit of what you were thinking and doing at the time.

Heard that J.C.Sturm had a book that was worthy of publishing - knew how to make books, had money - took a look, thought it great, so did partners, agreed to publish.

2 - Who or what was your main influence behind your decision to publish? These may include literary or non-literary influences.

Love poetry and good writing and books and the craft behind them.

3 - In your choice of authors was the main consideration for inclusion philosophical, literary or pragmatic?

Philosophical - I like "Authentic Voices" - very keen on Māori voices, 'Other' world views.

Pragmatic - "Who turned up at the door."

4 - "...and if there is still a number of commissioned works which seem to have been dreamed up by a sabotaging office-boy on an LSD trip, there are now each year a growing quantity of books which worthily add to our literature." Professor J.C. Reid from an article introducing *New Zealand Books in Print*, written in 1968. I interpret Reid's assessment as an indication of the rift between the acceptable 'worthy' literature as endorsed by academia, and the new wave of sabotaging office boys and girls who at that time commissioned publishers to put out their works, or simply published things themselves, and in many cases the work of their friends. Comment on this quote in relation to the 'Vanity Press' vs 'Real Publishing' debate.

"Vanity" is a nonsense in a tiny market - a lot if not all books need a financial boost in N.Z.

5 - Initially, was your focus outwardly cosmopolitan or inwardly New Zealand looking, and how has this emphasis changed over the years?

More NZ-looking at first - Has changed somewhat, would love to find a book, e.g. a novel, that would sell overseas. But still fiercely loyal to N.Z. (only want to go overseas for writer's benefit, and to survive financially).

6 - What were your methods of printing and distribution as a publisher? Did you receive any financial or other assistance from either public organisations, or private sponsorship?

Used local printer for first 30 or so books - had lots of public and private sponsorship - still went broke. Distributed myself at first, got national distributors after a year or so.

7 - How much of your publishing was commissioned and paid for (either fully or partially) by the author? Was your operation helped by the voluntary work of friends and family?

(a) Maybe a quarter was author-assisted
(b) H - U - G - E --- Voluntary help from family, friends and
   curious explorers.

8 - What has been the cost to you personally in terms of time, money and resources, of being involved in publishing in New Zealand? You may consider this in relation to more difficult areas such as relationships with friends, family etc. also.

Lost tens, maybe hundreds of thousands of dollars. Lost my non-work 'life' - work all the time. Lost contact with scores of friends and family. Work every night, every weekend. Severe strain on marriage.

9 - Where do you place yourself and your achievements as a publisher (and as a writer if applicable) in the history of the modern-day New Zealand literary scene? Do you

feel that your contribution has been adequately acknowledged?

(a) A tiny, insignificant blip on the landscape that has helped a few writers and hindered, I regret, a few too.
(b) No, I don't feel adequately acknowledged, but I can live with that!

R.S. Wellington, 2000.

Publisher: Sudden Valley Press.

John O'Connor, a poet who has been writing for many years and whose work has been widely anthologized. His S.V.P. is gaining recognition as one of the more stylish and interesting publishers of poetry volumes in recent times.

ALLISON, John, ***Both Roads Taken***, 1997, Poetry

ALLISON, John, ***Stone Moon Dark Water***, 1999, Poetry

FEA, Kenneth, ***On What is Not***, 1999, Poetry

GADD, Bernard, ***Stepping Off From Northland: Selected New Poems***, 1997, Poetry

GREGORY, David, ***Always Arriving***, 1997, Poetry

GREGORY, David, ***Frame of Mind***, 1999, Poetry

JACOBS, Helen, ***Pools Over Stone***, 1997, Poetry

JACOBS, Helen, ***The Usefulness of Singing***, 1999, Poetry

LINDSAY, Graham, *Legend of the Cool Secret*, 1999, Poetry

O'CONNOR, John, *As It Is: Poems, 1981 - 1996*, 1997, Poetry

O'CONNOR, John, *Particular Context*, 1999, Poetry

PIRIE, Mark, *Shoot*, 1999, Poetry

*All books between 150 and 200 copies.

1 - What was your initial reason for getting involved in publishing? Please try to think of this in the spirit of what you were thinking and doing at the time.

For me the decision to start Sudden Valley (with David Gregory as a mostly sleeping partner) came out of two background factors. One was that I couldn't get a press to publish my *As It Is*, apart from Hazard who wanted too much to do so. The other was a background in publishing.

As you can see from my C.V. (enclosed) I put out a couple of pamphlets in the 70s and a couple of books in the 80s (the latter under the Concept imprint). Basically Concept was a distributor - Ashley King - who made out he was a publisher.

Late 80s early 90s I also published 5 issues of a poetry journal titled *plainwraps* Then, in the mid-90s, the Canterbury Poets Collective (of which I was a co-organizer) put out its second local anthology *Voiceprints 2*, which I was involved with too.

Underlying this was a wish to start a small press, just for its own sake.

2 - Who or what was your main influence behind your decision to publish? These may include literary or non-literary influences.

I don't think there was anything apart from the answers to Q.1.

3 - In your choice of authors was the main consideration for inclusion philosophical, literary or pragmatic?

All 3.

Starting with <u>pragmatic</u>: you can only work with those who want to and can afford to. If poets have better options they'll take them up.

<u>Literary</u>: only to some extent. I have eclectic taste myself so I didn't have a problem with various styles / approaches to poetry. There had to be a literary standard, however, below which the books couldn't go.

<u>Philosophical</u>: not that it came up, but the only things I would have said no to would have been right-wing seeming texts. (i.e., anything that seemed to favour elites / power / capital. I expect a decent set of human values from S.V.P. authors.)

Overall, then, of all those mss available to S.V.P., rejections have been made on the grounds of literary standard. (I've missed one or two, also, because the author couldn't afford to pay part of the printing costs.)

4 - "...and if there is still a number of commissioned works which seem to have been dreamed up by a sabotaging office-boy on an LSD trip, there are now each year a growing quantity of books which worthily add to our literature." Professor J.C. Reid from an article introducing *New Zealand Books in Print*, written in 1968. I interpret Reid's assessment as an indication of the rift between the acceptable 'worthy' literature as endorsed by academia, and the new wave of sabotaging office boys and girls who at that time commissioned publishers to put out their works, or simply published things themselves, and in many cases the work of their friends. Comment on this quote in relation to the 'Vanity Press' vs 'Real Publishing' debate.

There's so much bullshit written about lit., and in this context in particular.

Comments that might be appropriate.

1) Academia was then in the more trad. mode of defending the old against the new.

2) This no longer seems to be the case. Good numbers of academics are on the lit-canon trip, e.g. Mark Williams (I think) in the intro to **Opening the Books** makes no secret of the sort of power he & his kind wield in his comments on bringing through women writers in the 70s & 80s. (No reference to quality, or audience and their response - just (as I recall) "we" decided this was going to happen. Instant product.)

<u>Note</u>: I'm not saying some of these writers are unworthy of status - but I am commenting on the <u>power</u> relationships that create that status.

It seems to me that academia has dropped its trad. defence of the old (against the new) for a quite different role: that of "cheer leaders" for a certain set of often new writers, mainly out of the university presses, and V.U.P. in particular. The counterpoint to this of course is that they try to marginalise &/or denigrate writers who are not part of that "establishment" - often the small press writer.

5 - Initially, was your focus outwardly cosmopolitan or inwardly New Zealand looking, and how has this emphasis changed over the years?

Always been a bit of both - maybe as the years have passed I've looked <u>more</u> inward. But I still maintain a reasonably broad focus.

6 - What were your methods of printing and distribution as a publisher? Did you receive any financial or other assistance from either public organisations, or private sponsorship

Printing - off-set or docutech.

Distribution - reciprocal arrangements with friends:

Auckland = Tony Beyer
Wellington/Dunedin = Mark Pirie
Christchurch = me
(all S.O.R. to shops)

Plus flyers to libraries and sales at our C.P.C. readings.

Only one of our 12 S.V.P. books (to date) has gained a C.N.Z. publishing grant - $1,300 for ***The Usefulness of Singing***, which was done on off-set.

Two of our books, ***On What is Not*** and ***Shoot***, got a $500 interest free loan from S.V.P. to help with printing. The rest is author paid. (Almost all the books have managed to cover their costs to date. Certainly S.V.P. got its $1,000 back - the rest to the authors. We are non-profit.)

7 - How much of your publishing was commissioned and paid for (either fully or partially) by the author? Was your operation helped by the voluntary work of friends and family?

1) See previous question.

2) Only a little. S.V.P. is pretty much a one-man-band. (I do, usually, get the authors to set out / lay out their work though. Lots of hand holding needed.)

8 - What has been the cost to you personally in terms of time, money and resources, of being involved in publishing in New Zealand? You may consider this in relation to more difficult areas such as relationships with friends, family etc. also.

Great cost in time. Money, not really - unless one counts what one could have earned by continuing in teaching.

However, that was a conscious decision about 10 years ago (to leave teaching and drive cabs over the weekend, thus freeing up time for writing, publishing etc.) I don't regret that decision.

Yes, it puts considerable strain on family life and on my health. (25 to 30 hours at night over the weekend, plus however many for poetry during the week. The change of sleep pattern doesn't help either).

9 - Where do you place yourself and your achievements as a publisher (and as a writer if applicable) in the history of the modern-day New Zealand literary scene? Do you feel that your contribution has been adequately acknowledged.

S.V.P. is a small press - but it's put out some very good work. It (& presses like it) add variety and I think some vitality to the scene.

As a writer: not really for me to judge. I think one of the big pitfalls for writers is comparing themselves with others. (Usually favourably). It leads to illusions about the "greatness" of one's work. (Even one S.V.P. poet thinks he's up there with Eliot & Rilke!). I try not to get on this track. Rather, I compare my work with my earlier work and try to see if I'm changing, making progress, etc.

I'd like to be more recognized of course (only human). But so much of that is political. Writing grants (or another at some point) would be very useful - even the small one I've had recently ($9,000) will help free up time. In fact it's a big help in that respect.

See Ken Fea's book ***On What is Not***, for instance. It's not the standard poetry volume at all.

J.O'C. Christchurch, 2000.

Publisher: Voice Press.

Lindsay Rabbitt is a writer and illustrator who extolled the virtues of minimalism and was active as a publisher in the 1970's and 80's. He now works as a journalist.

COCHRANE, Geoff, *Sea the Landsman Knows*, 1979, Poetry (300 copies)

ELSE, Chris, *Dreams of Pythagoras*, 1981, 10 stories (1000 copies)

JOHNSON, Mike, *The Palanquin Ropes*, 1983, Poetry (650 copies)

ORR, Bob, *Cargo*, 1983, Poetry (650 copies)

RABBITT, Lindsay, *Upagainstit*, 1983, Poetry (350 copies)

RABBITT, Lindsay, *On the Line*, 1985, Poetry, with drawings by Jane Pountney (350 copies)

RABBITT, Lindsay, ed., *Solstice*, 1978, Anthology, with Geoff Cochrane and V. Broome (300 copies)

SCOTT, Lewis, *Nothing but a Man*, 1980, Poetry (650 copies)

TAYLOR, Apirana, *Eyes of the Ruru*, 1979, Poetry (1000 copies)

TAYLOR, Apirana, et al., *3 Shades*, 1981, Poetry, with Lindsay Rabbitt and Lewis Scott, introduction by Alan Loney (1000 copies)

WATSON, Jean Catherine, *Flowers from Happyever*, 1980, Prose lyric (1200 copies)

1 - What was your initial reason for getting involved in publishing? Please try to think of this in the spirit of what you were thinking and doing at the time.

I left school early to take up an apprenticeship in hand and machine typography at the local "rag" in Alexandra, Central Otago. I didn't read literary books till my mid 20s, but was involved with the printed word in my day-to-day working life. I started writing in naive way in the mid 70s and started to meet people in the literary scene. My training as a printer gave me the knowledge of how to put books together, so it seemed a logical next step to want to produce them.

2 - Who or what was your main influence behind your decision to publish? These may include literary or non-literary influences.

The first poet I read was William Blake. I was then drawn to the Americans, namely minimalists, Robert Creeley and Cid Corman. Later on Ginsberg and in particular William Carlos Williams ("not in ideas, but in things").

3 - In your choice of authors was the main consideration for inclusion philosophical, literary or pragmatic?

I was open-minded and anything people showed me I would look at. I was learning as I went along and as I became more well-read my confidence grew. I called my little publishing outfit Voice Press because of the many "voices" I perceived in NZ literature. It also had the connotation of the spoken voice - the uniqueness of the individual human voice having its own peculiar rhythm.

4 - "...and if there is still a number of commissioned works which seem to have been dreamed up by a sabotaging office-boy on an LSD trip, there are now each year a growing quantity of books which worthily add to our literature." Professor J.C. Reid from an article introducing *New Zealand Books in Print*, written in 1968. I interpret Reid's assessment as an indication of the rift between the acceptable 'worthy' literature as endorsed

by academia, and the new wave of sabotaging office boys and girls who at that time commissioned publishers to put out their works, or simply published things themselves, and in many cases the work of their friends. Comment on this quote in relation to the 'Vanity Press' vs 'Real Publishing' debate.

Given the times, the 60's & 70's, that notion of an official or validated literature was in some ways what I was rebelling against. It wasn't only us (minor poets), people like Baxter had more or less started the rebellion before us.

5 - Initially, was your focus outwardly cosmopolitan or inwardly New Zealand looking, and how has this emphasis changed over the years?

Cosmo.

6 - What were your methods of printing and distribution as a publisher? Did you receive any financial or other assistance from either public organisations, or private sponsorship?

I did all the pre-press work - all but **Landsman** were printed on off-set - the other was on letterpress. Distribution was by Brick Row. About half the books received Literary Fund grants, otherwise I did it myself, subsidised by commercial jobs.

7 - How much of your publishing was commissioned and paid for (either fully or partially) by the author? Was your operation helped by the voluntary work of friends and family?

1. None.

2. Jill Brasell (my first wife) helped, as did Alan Loney. Alan and I did a lot of the design work and commercial printing projects together.

8 - What has been the cost to you personally in terms of time, money and resources, of being involved in publishing in New Zealand? You may consider this in relation to more difficult areas such as relationships with friends, family etc. also.

It didn't do anything for my finances, but it was an important process to move on to other things.

9 - Where do you place yourself and your achievements as a publisher (and as a writer if applicable) in the history of the modern-day New Zealand literary scene? Do you feel that your contribution has been adequately acknowledged.

I see the whole process of writing and publishing as an on-going one. I'm now a journalist and write about arts and culture, and while my *modus operandi* has changed, my earlier hunches about the need to record the different voices of our small country have not changed.

L.R. Kapiti, 2000.

Supplementary Bibliographies

These preliminary bibliographies (except in the case of E.S.A.W., which is complete) are included to give further indication of the type of books and authors these small presses published and their contribution to NZ literature. The emphasis is on the literary publications and is by no means comprehensive.

Publisher: The Bottle Press. Sam Hunt, et al. All these publications occurred between 1969 and 1971 and were about 200 copies per print run

HUNT, Sam, ***When Morning Comes (a flat fat blues)***, Poetry, cover by Robin White

HUNT, Sam, ***A Song About Her***, Poetry, cover by Robin White

HUNT, Sam, ***Postcard of a Cabbage Tree***, Poetry, cover by Robin White

HUNT, Sam, ***Bottle Creek Blues***, Poetry, cover with signatures by Bottle Creek residents

HUNT, Sam, *Letter to Jerusalem*, Poetry, cover by Robin White

BAXTER, James K., *Jerusalem Blues 2*, Poetry, cover by Robin White

CAMPBELL, Alistair, *Drinking Horn*, Poetry, cover by Robin White

LASENBY, Jack, *Over Makara*, Poetry, cover by Robin White

CAMPBELL, Alistair, *Walk the Black Path*, **As Triple P Press**

LASENBY, Jack, *Two Grandfathers*, Poetry

LASENBY, Jack, *A Poster Poem*, Poetry

HUNT, Sam, *Birth on Bottle Creek*, Poetry

HUNT, Sam, *Beware the Man*, Poetry, cover by Sam Hunt

HUNT, Sam, *Roadsong Paekakariki*, Poetry

Publisher: Coromandel Press. Barry Mitcalfe was a writer and political activist who was notable for his work on Maori poetry. He is also known for his children's stories, and the bibliography of his press shows his commitment to poetry and illustrated texts. He died in 1986.

BARRIER, D., *Such Feet Little Horse*, 1981, With illustrations from original paintings by Michael Illingworth

BROWN, R. F., *Gone, No Address*, 1982, With illustrations by Nigel Brown

BROWN, Robyn, **Cocoon Rooms**, 1979, With illustrations by Penny Atkinson

FREEMAN, Sue., **Fat Chance**, 1982

GREENWOOD, J., **Beach, Gulls, Dreamer**, 1984, With drawings by Eric Lee-Johnson and Sara Macdonald

MITCALFE, Barry, **Beach**, 1982

MITCALFE, Barry, **Country Road**, 1980, With illustrations by Mike Cogswell

MITCALFE, Barry, **Gulf**, 1980

MITCALFE, Barry, **Harvestman**, 1979, Poetry, with etchings by Susan Poff

MITCALFE, Barry, **Hey Hey Hey**, 1985, With illustrations by Annette Isbey

MITCALFE, Barry, **Look to the Land**, 1986

MITCALFE, Barry, **Maori**, 1981

MITCALFE, Barry, **The North**, 1981

MITCALFE, Barry, **Northland, New Zealand**, 1984

MITCALFE, Barry, **Pighunter**, 1980, With photography by Peter Warren

MITCALFE, Barry, **Sun, moon and stars**, 1982, With illustrations by Susan Poff

MITCALFE, Barry, **Uncle and Others**, 1979

MUTTON, Gary, ***The Haven and the Fire***, 1984, Poetry, with drawings by Barry Lett

PENDERGRAST, M., ***Raranga Whakairo***, 1984, Māori plaiting patterns

RIDDELL, Ron, ***Breathing Space***, 1986, Poetry, illustrated by Kate Riddell

WILLIAMS, Haare, ***Karanga***, 1981, With illustrations by Rei Hamon

---

Publisher: E.S.A.W. Michael O'Leary poet, novelist, artist, performance poet and bookshop / art gallery proprietor, O'Leary's career as a literary publisher covers twenty years. He works under two main imprints, The Earl of Seacliff Art Workshop and, since 1987, Miracle Mart Receiving, procured from Greg O'Brien in a corporate raid common during that time for a seven figure sum (O'Brien still has the uncashed cheque for $1,000,003 to prove it).

AMERY, Colin, ***Ten minutes to Midnight***, 1989, Rainbow Warrior history (800 copies)

BROWN, Nigel, ***Black Frame***, 1988 With Warwick Brown, commentary and poetry produced in conjunction with exhibition at Lopdell House, Titirangi in March, 1988 (100 copies)

DUNCAN, Grant, ***Away with Words***, 1986, Poetry (250 copies)

EGGLETON, David, ***After Tokyo***, 1987, Prose pieces with illustrations by Bryan Harold and Robin Conway (300 copies)

ELLIS, John, ***Loud Quiet Song***, 1997, Poetry (200 copies)

ENTWISLE, Peter, ***Elaine and Other Stories***, 1992, Prose (250 copies)

HARE, Brian, ***From and for Jesus***, 1998, Poetry (100 copies)

HENSHALL, Roberta, ed., ***The City Assails: New Auckland Writers***, 1987, Poetry (250 copies)

LAUBE, Judith, ***Limbo Dancing***, 1987, Poetry, with woodcuts by Kathryn Madill (250 copies)

O'LEARY, Michael, ***Flip Side of the Ballad of John and Yoko***, 1980 1999, Poetry (100 copies) reprint (100 copies)

O'LEARY, Michael, ***Ten Sonnets: Myths and Legends of Love***, 1984, Poetry (10 copies)

O'LEARY, Michael, ***Straight: a Novel in the Irish-Maori Tradition***, 1984 & 1985, Novel, illustrated by Gregory O'Brien (100 copies) reprint (150 copies)

O'LEARY, Michael, ***Out of It***, 1987, Novel, collages by Thomas Hickey, cover by Iain Sharp (250 copies)

O'LEARY, Michael, ***Hala e Kolo ni Mo Ha Lanu***, 1989, Children's story, translated into Tongan by Kahoa Corbett, drawings by Lena Patience (100 copies)

O'LEARY, Michael, ***The Irish Annals of New Zealand***, 1991 & 1997, Novel, cover by Sean Manning, (300 copies) new edition (50) in Celtic script

O'LEARY, Michael, ***Kia Aroha***, 1992, Poetry with Bill Dacker (7 copies)

O'LEARY, Michael, *He Waiatanui kia Aroha*, 1993, Poetry (3 copies)

O'LEARY, Michael, *Seens from the Irish Annals*, 1993, Drawings, by Michael O'Leary and Wayne Seyb inspired by the novel *The Irish Annals of New Zealand* (10 copies)

O'LEARY, Michael, *Scrapbook*, 1998, Collection of articles and ephemera by and about the author and E.S.A.W. (25 copies)

O'LEARY, Michael, ed., *Wrapper*, 1992, Anthology of new and established writers illustrated by Nigel Brown and Gregory O'Brien (300 copies)

O'LEARY, Michael, ed., *Waiting for a Train of Thought,* 1998, Poetry and prose with students from the editor's Creative Writing course at Whitireia (25 copies)

O'LEARY, Michael, ed., *9 Seasons*, 1998, Poetry and prose with students from the editor's Creative Writing course at Whitireia (25 copies)

O'SHAUGHNESSEY, M. and BLUNT, I., *The Arraignment of Dr. Ley*, 1989, Satire (50 copies), 1989 reprint (100 copies)

PARKER, Glyn, *Passion*, 1990, Novel (1500 copies)

PATERSON, Alistair, *Incantations for Warriors*, 1987, Poetry, limited edition, signed and numbered copies, with 21 drawings by Roy Dalgarno (500 copies)

RENNIE, Niel, *The Super Man*, 1988, Novel (300 copies)

RIDDELL, Ron, *Elegy in Memory of Barry Mitcalfe*, 1987, Poetry (250 copies)

RIDDELL, Ron, ***How to Eat a Hotdog on the Main Street of Thames***, 1990, Poetry, illustrated by Zuna Wright (100 copies)

ROMANIUK, Janni, ***The Quest***, 1990, Poetry (200 copies)

SMITHER, Elizabeth, ***Gorilla / Guerrilla***, 1986, Poetry, illustrated by Gregory O'Brien, numbered and signed by author and artist (250 copies)

TAIT, Peter, ***Ain't No Cat***, 1989, Poetry (100 copies)

YATES, Nigel, ***Dunedin: an Essay***, 1993, Second edition of photographic book numbered copies (100 copies)

AS MIRACLE MART RECEIVING / E.S.A.W.

JENSEN, Kai, ***Hans Urlich Rudel and His Stuka***, 1989, Poetry (200 copies)

LIPSCHUTZ, Michael, ***The Break of the Twig and the Fall of the Leaf***, 1987, Poetry (250 copies)

O'LEARY, Michael, ***Before and After***, 1987, Poetry and prose (250 copies)

O'LEARY, Michael, ***Livin' ina Aucklan'***, 1988, Poetry illustrated by John Pule (100 copies)

Publisher: New Womens Press. Wendy Harrex is a respected editor and in 1993 took over the helm at Otago University Press.

CHALMERS, Alexandria, ***The Wintering House***, 1989, Novel

CHARMAN, Janet, *2 Deaths in 1 Night*, 1987, Poetry

CHERRY, Frances, *The Daughter-in-Law and other Stories*, 1986, Short stories

CHERRY, Frances, *Dancing with Strings*, 1989, Fiction

CHERRY, Frances, *The Widowhood of Jacki Bates*, 1991, Fiction

COWLEY, Joy, *Nest in a Falling Tree*, 1984, Novel

CRAVEN, Candis, *Women's Studies*, 1985, A New Zealand handbook

DUNSFORD, Cathie, ed., *The Exploding Frangpani*, 1990, Lesbian writing from Australia and New Zealand, with S. Hawthorne

DUNSFORD, Cathie, ed., *New Women's Fiction*, 1986, Anthology

ELLMERS, Judith, *Born Beneath a Rainbow*, Memoir

HARREX, Wendy, ed., *New Women's Fiction*, 1991, With L. Ferrari

HYDE, Robin, *Dragon Rampant*, 1984, Novel

HYDE, Robin, *Nor the Years Condemn*, 1986, Novel, P. Bunkle, L. Hardy, J. Matthews, eds.

HYDE, Robin, *Wednesday's Children*, 1989, Novel

IP, Manying, ed., *Home Away From Home*, 1990, Life stories of Chinese women in N.Z.

JOHNSON, Stephanie, **Crimes of Neglect**, 1992, Fiction

JOHNSON, Stephanie, **The Glass Whittler**, 1988, Short stories

KEITH, Sheridan, **Animal Passions**, 1992, Novel

KEITH, Sheridan, **Shallow are the Smiles at the Supermarket**, 1991, Fiction

LANGKILDE CHRISTIE, Poula, **Candles and Canvas**

MACFARLANE, Anne, **Feet Across America**, 1987, With illustrations by Vanya Lowry

MAKERETI, **The Old-time Maori**, Memoir and legends, introduced by Ngahuia Te Awekotuku

McLEOD, Aorewa, ed., **New Women's Fiction**, 1988, Fiction, introduced by Ngahuia Te Awekotuku

MOUNTJOY, Lora, **Deep Breathing**, 1984, Fiction

OWENS, Jacqueline, **Bluest Moon**, 1990, Fiction

PAUL, Mary, ed., **New Women's Fiction**, 1989, Fiction, with Marion Rae

ROSIER, Pat, **Broadsheet**, 1992, 20 years of Broadsheet Magazine

STEWART, Terry, **Invisible Families**, 1993, Resource for families with gay and lesbian children

SUTHERLAND, Margaret, **The Love Contract**, 1984

SVENSSON, Carin, *One Plain, One Purl*, 1989, Stories of a girlhood

SVENSSON, Carin, *An Unusually Clumsy Lover*, 1991

TE AWEKOTUKU, Ngahuia, *Mana Wahine Maori*, 1991, Selected writing on Māori women's art, culture etc.

TE AWEKOTUKU, Ngahuia, *Tahuri*, 1989, Short stories

VON REICHE, Momoe Malietoa, *Tai: Heart of a Tree*, 1988, Poetry

---

Publisher: Alister Taylor. One of the most controversial and enduring of our small press publishers, Taylor has married aesthetic book production with an uncanny knack of knowing 'what' to publish ahead of any given trend. His contribution to New Zealand literature has often been obscured, but it is extensive and covers more than three decades of innovation.

ALTERNATIVE WRITING GROUP, *The First, Last and Complete Patricia Bartlett Cookbook and Household Physician or Practical Knowledge for the People* , 1972, With F.B. Dickerson

BARR, Jim, *The Muldoon Annual Jokebook*, 1971, With Alister Taylor

BAXTER, James K., *James K Baxter: 1926 - 1972, a memorial volume*, 1972

BOOTH, Pat, *Son's of the Sword*, 1993, A novel of the Pacific war

CAMERON, Miriam, ***In Defence of Children: a book for the International Year of the Child in New Zealand***, 1980, With Jan Mudrovich and Tim Shadbolt, introduced by Rewi Alley

CAMPBELL, Alistair, ***Collected Poems: 1947 - 1981***, 1981, Poetry

CODDINGTON, Deborah, ***Liberty Belle: Ten Years of Writing***, 1998, Introduction by Lindsay Perigo

CURNOW, Heather, ***The Life and Art of William Strutt, 1825 - 1915***, 1980

GEIRINGER, Erich, ***The Lex Augusta***, 1979

GRAMAPHONE, Malcolm, ***The Brewer's Bible***, 1973, Home brewing guide

HACKFORTH -JONES, Jocelyn , ***Augustus Earle, Travel Artist*** , 1980, Paintings and drawings in the Rex Nan Kivell Collection, National Library of Australia

HUNT, Sam, ***From Bottle Creek***, 1972, Poetry

HUNT, Sam, ***Time to Ride***, 1975, Poetry

KING, Michael, ***Moko: Maori Tattooing in the 20th Century***, 1972, With photographs by Marti Friedlander

KRIEGLER, Lyn, ***Legend of the Kiwi***, 1981, Retold and illustrated

MANSFIELD, Katherine, ***Candle Fairy: Stories, Fairy Tales and Verse for Children***, 1992, Illustrated by Gabriella Klepatski, (compiled, edited and designed by Alister Taylor; calligraphy by Alison Furminger)

McLEOD, Rosemary, ***Rosemary McLeod's Bedside Book***, 1981, Satire

MORRISON, Robin, ***The South Island of New Zealand from the Road***, 1981, Photography

SHADBOLT, Tim, ***Bullshit and Jellybeans***, 1971, Political comment

SIMPSON, Tony, ***Riri Pakeha: the White Man's Anger***, 1979, Political comment

SUSSEX, Marian, ***The Magic Billy***, 1981, Illustrated by the author

TAYLOR, Alister, ***C.F. Goldie: Famous Maori Leaders of New Zealand***, 1981, Te Arawa, Nga Puhi, Ngati Hao, Ngati Parekawa, Tuhourangi, Ngati Raukawa, Nga Te Ata, Ngati Manunui, Ngati Tuwharetoa

TAYLOR, Alister, ***The Little Red Schoolbook***, 1969, 1960's 'cultural' revolution

TAYLOR, Alister, ed., ***The Third New Zealand Whole Earth Catalogue***, 1977, With Deborah McCormack and William Gruar

TE RAUPARAHA, Tamihana, ***Life and Times of Te Rauparaha by his son, Tamihana***, 1980, Edited by Peter Butler

WELCH, Chris, ***Hendrix: a Biography***, 1973, Designed by Pearce Marchbank

WESTRA, Ans, ***Notes on the Country I Live in***, 1972, Photography, with text by James K Baxter and Tim Shadbolt

WHITE, Robin, ***Robin White, New Zealand Painter***, 1981, Compiled by Alister and Deborah Coddingham

WILKES, Owen, ed., ***First New Zealand Whole Earth Catalogue***, 1972, Alternative lifestyle writings

YOUNG, Rose, ***G.F. von Tempsky, artist and adventurer***, 1981, With Heather Curnow and Michael King

Statistics and Tables

TABLE - 1
Number of titles published by surveyed small presses
1970 - 1979

	70	71	72	73	74	75	76	77	78	79
Amphedesma	1	2	2	2	-	1	-	-	-	-
Bard & Gulf	-	-	-	-	-	-	-	-	1	2
Black Robin	-	-	-	-	-	-	-	-	-	-
Brick Row	-	-	-	-	-	-	-	-	-	-
Bumper	-	-	-	-	-	-	-	-	-	-
Caveman	-	5	9	5	6	4	2	2	2	1
E.S.A.W.	-	-	-	-	-	-	-	-	-	-
Hallard	-	-	-	-	-	-	-	-	-	-
Hard Echo	-	-	-	-	-	-	-	-	-	-
Hawk	-	-	-	-	-	2	3	5	4	2
HeadworX	-	-	-	-	-	-	-	-	-	-
Huia	-	-	-	-	-	-	-	-	-	-
M.M.R.	-	-	-	-	-	-	-	-	-	-
Montgomery	-	3	2	1	-	-	-	-	-	-
Nag	1	1	1	1	-	-	1	-	-	2
One-Eyed	-	-	-	1	-	-	-	1	-	-
Original	-	-	-	-	-	-	-	-	1	-
Pemmican	-	-	-	-	-	-	-	-	-	-
Puriri	-	-	-	-	-	-	-	-	-	-
Spiral	-	-	-	-	-	-	1	-	-	-
Sudden Valley	-	-	-	-	-	-	-	-	-	-

TABLE - 1 cont.
Number of titles published by surveyed small presses 1980 - 1989

	80	81	82	83	84	85	86	87	88	89
Amphedesma	-	-	-	-	-	-	-	-	-	-
Bard & Gulf	1	-	2	1	-	1	-	-	-	-
Black Robin	-	-	-	-	2	2	1	2	-	2
Brick Row	-	1	2	2	-	-	2	-	1	1
Bumper	-	-	-	-	-	-	-	-	-	-
Caveman	5	5	1	1	-	-	-	-	-	-
E.S.A.W.	1	-	-	-	2	1	1	7	3	5
Hallard	2	3	1	-	1	2	1	1	2	2
Hard Echo	1	3	2	3	7	7	5	3	1	1
Hawk	1	-	2	1	-	-	-	-	-	-
HeadworX	-	-	-	-	-	-	-	-	-	-
Huia	-	-	-	-	-	-	-	-	-	-
M.M.R.	-	-	-	-	-	-	1	1	3	-
Montgomery	-	-	-	-	-	-	-	-	-	-
Nag	-	1	-	1	-	2	1	1	2	1
One-Eyed	1	1	1	-	-	1	-	5	-	-
Original	-	-	-	-	-	2	-	-	2	7
Pemmican	-	-	-	-	-	-	-	-	-	-
Puriri	1	4	2	3	2	1	-	3	1	3
Spiral	-	-	1	2	-	2	1	2	-	-
Sudden Valley	-	-	-	-	-	-	-	-	-	-

TABLE - 1 cont.
Number of titles published by surveyed small presses
1990 - 1999

	90	91	92	93	94	95	96	97	98	99
Amphedesma	-	-	-	-	-	-	-	-	-	-
Bard & Gulf	-	-	-	-	-	-	-	-	-	-
Black Robin	-	-	-	-	-	-	-	-	-	-
Brick Row	1	2	-	2	2	-	-	1	1	-
Bumper	-	-	-	-	1	-	-	-	7	6
Caveman	-	-	-	-	-	-	-	-	-	-
E.S.A.W.	2	1	3	3	-	-	-	2	4	1
Hallard	1	2	2	-	-	2	1	-	2	2
Hard Echo	-	1	-	-	-	-	-	-	-	-
Hawk	-	-	-	-	-	-	-	-	-	-
HeadworX	-	-	-	-	-	-	-	-	4	4
Huia	-	-	-	-	1	2	2	3	2	4
M.M.R.	3	-	-	-	-	-	4	2	3	2
Montgomery	-	-	-	-	-	-	-	-	-	-
Nag	2	-	2	1	-	2	-	3	2	1
One-Eyed	1	-	-	-	-	-	-	-	-	-
Original	1	1	1	1	3	2	1	8	8	11
Pemmican	-	-	-	-	-	-	-	2	5	3
Puriri	3	4	-	3	1	2	1	2	1	1
Spiral	1	-	1	1	-	-	-	-	-	2
Sudden Valley	-	-	-	-	-	-	-	5	-	7

TABLE - 2

Longevity of small presses surveyed, showing years when publishing between 1970 and 2000

	1970	1975	1980	1985	1990	1995	2000
Amphedesma	■	■					
Bard & Gulf			■	■			
Black Robin				■	■		
Brick Row			■	■		■	■
Bumper						■	■
Caveman		■	■				
E.S.A.W.			■	■	■	■	■
Hallard			■	■	■	■	■
Hard Echo			■	■	■		
Hawk		■	■				
HeadworX							■
Huia						■	■
M.M.R.				■	■	■	■
Montgomery		■					
Nag's Head	■	■	■	■	■		■
One-Eyed		■	■	■	■		
Original			■	■	■	■	■
Pemmican							■
Puriri			■	■	■	■	■
Spiral		■			■		
Steele Roberts						■	■
Sudden Valley						■	■

TABLE - 3

Numbers of literary works published in relation to the overall number of publications in New Zealand, 1969 to 1982 and 1988 to 1998.
SP=The Small Presses represented in the bibliographies of the publishers in this survey.

| Year | General | | Literature | | |
	Total Publish	Total Lit.	Books	Pamphlets	SP
1969	1274	*59*	18	41	7
1970	1580	*108*	57	51	9
1971	1324	*75*	35	40	17
1972	1215	*69*	36	33	14
1973	1339	*97*	56	41	10
1974	1598	*83*	61	22	6
1975	1887	*106*	70	36	7
1976	1835	*132*	71	61	7
1977	1939	*130*	56	74	8
1978	2079	*178*	56	122	8
1979	2496	*151*	69	82	7
1980	2850	*134*	47	87	13
1981	2499	*153*	79	74	18
1982	1588	*129*	64	65	14
1988	5449				17
1989	5625				22
1990	5021				15
1991	5367				11
1992	6461				8
1993	6308				11
1994	5973				8
1995	6818				10
1996	9430				9
1997	8536				28
1998	8579				39

General figures from the N.Z. National Bibliography. (Those from 1988 onwards are distorted because they include catch-up figures from previous years)

Small press figures from survey bibliographies.

TABLE - 4

Creative New Zealand (and previous NZ Literary Fund) - Number of grants per year 1977 to 1999* showing percentages of funding for each category.

A = University Presses

B = Established or Commercial Presses

C = Small Presses which received funding (not just the ones surveyed in this study).

YEAR	A			B			C		
			%			%			%
1977	2	=	12.5	6	=	37.5	8	=	50
1978	6	=	35	3	=	18	8	=	47
1979	3	=	19	4	=	25	9	=	56
1980	4	=	36	2	=	19	5	=	45
1981	12	=	37.5	9	=	28.5	11	=	34
1982	7	=	50	2	=	15	5	=	35
1983	7	=	36	6	=	32	6	=	32
1984	5	=	25	4	=	20	11	=	55
1986	31	=	37.5	22	=	26.5	30	=	36
1987	7	=	54	3	=	23	3	=	23
1988	12	=	39	6	=	19	13	=	42
1992	20	=	30	32	=	48	15	=	22
1992	3	=	11	17	=	60	8	=	29
1993	9	=	24	15	=	39	14	=	37
1994	4	=	9.5	18	=	42.5	20	=	48
1995	13	=	42	11	=	35	7	=	23
1996	7	=	28	12	=	48	6	=	24
1997	12	=	38.5	11	=	35.5	8	=	26
1998	20	=	42.5	14	=	29.5	13	=	28
1999	5	=	25	10	=	50	5	=	25

* Figures not available for 1989-1991

Table -5

Presses publishing more than one author (published by other presses surveyed)

Amphedesma	Bill Manhire	Alan Brunton, Dennis List, Bill Manhire, Bob Orr, Ian Wedde
Black Robin Press	Bill Wieben	Ruth Gilbert, Lindsay Rabbitt
Brick Row	Oz Kraus	Bernard Gadd, Roger Horrocks, Michael Morrisey, Denys Trussell, Alistair Paterson, M.K. Joseph, Harvey McQueen
Bumper Books	Alan Brunton	Alan Brunton, G.J. Melling
Caveman Press	Trevor Reeves	Tony Beyer, Murray Edmond, Riemke Ensing, Dennis List, Alan Loney, G.J. Melling, Barry Mitcalfe, Michael Morrisey, Peter Olds, Hone Tuwhare
E.S.A.W.	Michael O'Leary	Nigel Brown, David Eggleton, Michael O'Leary, Iain Sharp, Alistair Paterson, Ron Riddell, Greg O'Brien, Elizabeth Smither
Hallard Press	Bernard Gadd	Bernard Gadd, M.K. Joseph, John O'Connor
Hard Echo Press	Warwick Jordan	Tony Beyer, David Howard, Mike Johnson, Iain Sharp, Paddy Richardson
Hawk Press	Alan Loney	Alan Brunton, Murray Edmond, Graham Lindsay, Alan Loney, Bill Manhire, Bob Orr, Elizabeth Smither, Lewis Scott, Ian Wedde, Stephen Oliver
HeadworX	Mark Pirie	Tony Beyer, Riemke Ensing, Harvey McQueen, Stephen Oliver, Harry Ricketts, Lewis Scott, Vivienne Plumb
M.M.R.	Greg O'Brien	Greg O'Brien, Elizabeth Smither, Chris Orsman, Bill Manhire
Montgomery Press	Peter Olds	Peter Olds, John Gibb
Nags Head Press	Bob Gormack	David Howard, Helen Shaw
One-Eyed Press	Chris Moisa	Peter Olds, Iain Sharp
Original Books	Niel Wright	Dennis List, Michael O'Leary, Harry Ricketts
Pemmican Press	Chris Orsman	Nigel Brown, Chris Orsman, Bill Manhire, Harry Ricketts, Vivienne Plumb
Prometheus Press	Donald Kerr	Riemke Ensing, Geoffrey de Montalk
Puriri Press	John Denny	Alan Loney, Greg O'Brien, Ron Riddell, Helen Shaw
Spiral Collective	Heather McPherson	Frances Cherry, J.C. Sturm
Steele Roberts	Roger Steele	Frances Cherry, J.C. Sturm, Hone Tuwhare, Paddy Richardson
Sudden Valley Press	John O'Connor	Bernard Gadd, Graham Lindsay
Voice Press	Lindsay Rabbitt	Mike Johnson, Bob Orr, Lindsay Rabbitt, Lewis Scott, Apirana Taylor

Bibliography

Andersen, Johannes. 'Early Printing in New Zealand'. In *A History of Printing in New Zealand.* Wellington: Richard Alexander McKay for the Wellington Club of Printing House Craftsmen, 1940.

Bagnall, A.G. (ed.). *New Zealand National Bibliography to the Year 1960.* Volume 1: To 1899. Wellington: P.D. Hasselberg, Government Printer, 1980.

Baxter, James K. *The Man on the Horse.* Dunedin: University of Otago Press, 1967.

Beatles. *Sergeant Pepper's Lonely Hearts Club Band.* London: Parlophone Records, 1967 (back of album cover)

Binney, Judith, Gillian Chaplin and Craig Wallace. *Mihaia: The Prophet Rua Kenana and His Community at Maungapohatu.* Wellington: Oxford University Press, 1979.

Bottle Creek: Exhibition Booklet. Wellington: Porirua Museum of Arts and Cultures, 1998.

Brunton, Alan, Murray Edmond and Michele Leggott (eds.). *Big Smoke: New Zealand Poems 1960 - 1975.* Auckland: Auckland University Press, 2000.

Bukowski, Charles. *Shakespeare Never Did This.* Santa Rosa: Black Sparrow Press, 1995.

Calder-Marshall, Arthur. *The Book Front.* London: The Bodley Head, 1948.

Carey, Rosalie. *A Theatre in the House: The Carey's Globe.* Dunedin: University of Otago Press, 1999.

Chapple, L.J.B. *A Bibliographical Brochure containing Addenda and Corrigenda to extant Bibliographies of New Zealand Literature.* Dunedin and Wellington: A.H. and A.W. Reed, 1938.

Cohen, Leonard. *Beautiful Losers.* London: Jonathan Cape, 1970.

Cohen, Leonard. *The Energy of Slaves.* London: Jonathan Cape, 1972.

Coleridge, Kathleen and Roderick Cave. *Early Printing in New Zealand.* Wellington: Department of Librarianship, Victoria University of Wellington, 1989.

Collie, Barbara (ed.). *New Zealand Books in Print 1970.* Wellington: New Zealand Book Publishers Association, 1970.

Curnow, Allen (ed.). *A Book of New Zealand Verse 1923 - 1945.* Christchurch: Caxton, 1945.

Curwen, Peter J. *The UK Publishing Industry.* Oxford, Pergamon Press, 1981.

Dacker, Bill. *Te Mamae me te Aroha: The Pain and the Love.* Dunedin: University of Otago Press in Association with the Dunedin City Council, 1994.

Denholm, Michael. *Small Press Publishing in Australia: the early 1970's.* Sydney: Second Back Row Press, 1979.

Denholm, Michael. *Small Press Publishing in Australia: the late 1970's to the mid to late 1980's, Volume 2.* Victoria: Footprint, 1991.

Dennison, Sally. *(Alternative) Literary Publishing: Five Modern Histories.* Iowa City: University of Iowa Press, 1984.

Drabble, Margaret (ed). *The Oxford Companion to English Literature.* 5th ed., (1st TSP Impression). Oxford: Oxford University Press, 1996.

Dylan, Bob. *Writings and Drawings of Bob Dylan.* London: Jonathan Cape, 1973.

Gifkins, Michael. 'Bookmarks'. *New Zealand Listener,* 5 March, 1990, p.129.

Glue, W.A. *History of the Government Printing Office.* Wellington: R.E. Owen, Government Printer, 1966.

Griffith, Penny, Ross Harvey, and Keith Maslen (eds.). *Book & Print in New Zealand: A Guide to Print Culture in Aotearoa.* Wellington: Victoria University Press, 1997.

Hopkins, Jerry. *Yoko Ono: A biography.* London: Sidgwick & Jackson, 1987.

Hunt, Janet. *Hone Tuwhare: A Biography.* Auckland: Godwit, 1998.

Kilgour, Frederick G. *The Evolution of the Book.* New York: Oxford University Press, 1998.

Lennon, John and Yoko Ono. *The Lennon Tapes.* London: British Broadcasting Corporation, 1981.

Lennon, John. *A Spaniard in the Works.* London: Jonathan Cape, 1965.

Lennon, John. *John Lennon in His Own Write.* London: Jonathan Cape, 1964.

Library Exhibition of Small Presses, Nov. 1977 - April 1978. Wellington: The New Zealand Book Council, 1977.

Lowry, Malcolm. *Selected Poems of Malcolm Lowry.* San Francisco: City Lights Books, 1962.

Manhire, Bill. *Doubtful Sounds.* Wellington: Victoria University Press, 2000.

Mann, Peter H. *Book Publishing, Book Selling and Book Reading: A Report to the Book Marketing Council of The Publishers Association.* London: Book Marketing Council, 1979.

Murray, Stuart. *Never a Soul at Home: New Zealand Literary Nationalism and the 1930's.* Wellington: Victoria University Press, 1998.

Myers, Robin and Michael Harris (eds.). *The Stationer's Company and the Book Trade, 1550 - 1990.* Winchester: St. Paul's Bibliographies, 1997.

Norrie, Ian. *Mumby's Publishing and Bookselling in the Twentieth Century.* 6th ed. London: Bell & Hyman, 1982.

O'Brien, Gregory. *Hotere; Out the Black Window: Ralph Hotere's work with NZ Poets.* Wellington: Godwit, in association with City Gallery, 1997.

O'Leary, Michael. *Flip Side of the Ballad of John and Yoko.* Auckland: E.S.A.W., 1980.

Paris Review. Paris: The Paris Review, (Spring 1973).

Park, Iris M. *New Zealand Periodicals of Literary Interest.* Wellington: Library School, National Library Service, 1962.

Paul, Janet and John Mansfield Thomson. *Landmarks in New Zealand Publishing; Blackwood & Janet Paul 1945 - 1968.* Wellington: National Library Gallery, 1995.

Pirie, Mark (ed). *The NeXt Wave.* Dunedin: University of Otago Press, 1998.

Robinson, Roger and Nelson Wattie (eds.). *The Oxford Companion to New Zealand Literature.* Melbourne: Oxford University Press, 1998.

Rohmer, Richard. ***Canadian Publishers & Canadian Publishing.*** Ontario: Ministry of the Attorney General, 1973.

Schroder, J.H.E. ***Second Appearances.*** Wellington: A.H. & A.W. Reed, 1959.

Shepard, Deborah. ***Reframing Women: a history of New Zealand film.*** Auckland: Harper Collins, 2000.

Smithyman, Kendrick. ***A Way of Saying: A Study of New Zealand Poetry.*** Auckland: Collins, 1965.

Sturm, Terry (ed.). ***The Oxford History of New Zealand Literature in English.*** 2nd ed. Auckland: Oxford University Press, 1998.

Traue, J.E. 'But Why Mulgan, Marris and Schroder? : the Mutation of the Local Newspaper in New Zealand's Colonial Print Culture'. ***BSANZ Bulletin***, vol.21 no.2, (1997), 107 - 115.

Vennell, O. St J. ***Patronage and New Zealand Literature.*** Wellington: Department of Internal Affairs, 1976.

Ward, Audrey & Philip. ***The Small Publisher: A Manual & Case Studies.*** New York: The Oleander Press, 1979.

West, James L.W. ***American Authors and the Literary Marketplace since 1900.*** Philadelphia: University of Pennsylvania Press, 1988.

Williams, Herbert W. ***A Bibliography of Printed Maori to 1900.*** Wellington: W.A.G. Skinner, Government Printer, 1924.

Williams, Herbert W. ***A Dictionary of the Maori Language.*** 7th ed. Wellington: Government Printing Office, 1971.

Williams Mark, 'Landfall: New Zealand's Longest-Running Literary Magazine,' ***The Poet's Voice.*** (Salzburg) Vol. 2, No. 1, (June 1995).

Woolf, Leonard. ***Beginning Again: An Autobiography of the Years 1911 to 1918.*** London: The Hogarth Press, 1964.

Wright, F.W. Nielsen. ***Blood in Her Cup: a History of the Muse in Aotearoa.*** Wellington: Cultural and Political Booklets, 1996.

Yate, William. ***An Account of New Zealand; and of the Formation and Progress of the Church Missionary Society's mission in the Northern Island.*** London: Seely and Burnside, 1835.